# LSWR

This book serves as a tribute to all the staff who have served the old LSWR during the past 150 years.

Overleaf
**The Bulleid 'West Country' class Pacifics were introduced in 1945. The first of this class, No 21C101 (BR No 34001) *Exeter*, speeds through Sherborne with a down West of England express, in the early days of nationalisation in 1948.** L&GPR (13970)

# LSWR

**LONDON**

**IAN ALLAN LTD**

B.K. Cooper & R. Antell

# A Tribute to the London & South Western Railway

Cover:
**A double-headed West of England express passes a down special in Weybridge Cutting.** From a painting by George F. Heiron

Back Cover, top:
**Class 442 No 2401 climbs Hinton Bank on a Bournemouth-Brockenhurst test run in February 1988.** Brian Denton

Back Cover, bottom:
**Preserved 'T9' 4-4-0 No 30120 leaves Meadstead & Four Marks with a train for Alton in 1986.** A. Ginno

First published 1988

ISBN 0 7110 1780 8

Published by Ian Allan Ltd, Shepperton, Surrey; and printed by Ian Allan Printing Ltd at their works at Coombelands in Runnymede, England

All uncredited photographs are from the Robert Antell Collection

Photographs from the L&GRP Collection are courtesy of David & Charles. Photographs credited to L&GRP and Real Photographs are available from:
    The Real Photographs Co
    Coombelands House,
    Coombelands Lane, Addlestone,
    Weybridge, Surrey KT15 1HY

**Acknowledgements:**
Grateful thanks go to all who have given help on this project, especially to the staff at Ian Allan Printing, Real Photographs, Bill Waylett, R. Lifford, Mr and Mrs E. J. Antell and W. F. Ottaway.

Also thanks go to Mr F. Burridge of the Dalkeith Publishing Co, Bournemouth, for the use of their Reproduction Railway Posters, and to John Slater, Editor of the *Railway Magazine*, for the use of some early illustrations.

# Contents

## THE YEARS OF GROWTH

## THE SOUTHERN YEARS

## NATIONALISATION

## APPENDICES

# The Years of Growth

**Yeovil Town**

# A Railway to Southampton

In the days of sail the passage of the English Channel for ships bound for the River Thames was often a struggle against wind and weather. During the Napoleonic wars the risk of interception and search by enemy vessels was another hazard. In those troubled times there was a scheme for an overland route to London by canal from Spithead, bypassing the Straits of Dover, but technical problems were soon discovered and the idea was dropped.

In 1825, with memories of the Napoleonic wars still very much alive, the example of the Stockton & Darlington Railway inspired the idea of connecting Southampton with London by railway. A line nearly 80 miles long was an audacious proposal at the time, apart from which navigation on Southampton Water was tricky for sailing ships and port facilities were poor. Southampton had known alternating periods of activity and decline. Steam power, both in ships and on land, would soon change its fortunes dramatically but that seemed visionary in 1825. There were more who scoffed at the idea of a railway than supported it.

By the next decade the situation had changed. The opening of the Liverpool & Manchester Railway had sparked enthusiasm for railway projects. A Southampton MP, Mr A. R. Dottin, held a private meeting on 26 February 1831, at which funds for setting up a company were subscribed and an engineer was appointed. He was Francis Giles, who had surveyed the route of the proposed Spithead to London canal. Soon afterwards, on 6 April 1831, a public meeting enthusiastically approved a proposal for a railway from Southampton to London, coupled with the building of new docks. The two must go hand in hand, said the Chairman, Col George Henderson, who described the condition of the docks as 'deplorable'. A prospectus of the enterprise was published in which it was described as the Southampton, London & Branch Railway & Dock Company. Before a Bill was presented to Parliament, however, the docks development was separated from the railway and became the responsibility of a new company, again with Giles as engineer.

At a meeting on 11 July 1832 it was explained that the 'branch' in the title referred to 'a contemplated junction by a railway extending to Bath and Bristol' and it was pointed out that 'the bend which is observable in our line at Basingstoke was mainly suggested with a view to facilitate that junction'. It was recommended, however, that the branch project should be omitted from the Bill for the Southampton-London line and be made the subject of a separate application. The revised Bill went before Parliament in the session of 1834 and the London & Southampton Railway Company (L&SR) was incorporated by an Act of 25 July in the same year. At the first general meeting of the new company on 24 October 1834 it was reported that work on building the line had already begun.

The question of a line to Bath and Bristol came up again at the meeting on 27 February 1835 and it was proposed to consider incorporating a Basing & Bath Railway Company with the London & Southampton. When the Great Western Railway's Bill for a line from Bristol to London was before Parliament, it was opposed by the London & Southampton, but after both schemes had been debated for 46 days the Great Western line was authorised. The London & Southampton had to abandon its cherished ambition of dominating the rail outlet from London to the West. This defeat rankled. In announcing it to the shareholders the Chairman virtually accused the Great Western supporters of mounting a 'dirty tricks' campaign, although in more dignified language, speaking of 'gross misrepresentations which had been industriously propagated to the prejudice of the Southampton Railway'. He asserted that the proceedings had proved the superiority of the Basing & Bath line, in spite of which 'the promoters of the Great Western Line have succeeded, by means unlooked for, as unprecedented, in obtaining a vote in favour of their project'. Referring to the episode nearly 50 years later in his London & South Western history, *A Royal Road*, Sam Fay claimed that the 'high-sounding name of Great Western, and the fact that it was described as the Direct Bristol Railway, gained many supporters and the line became the favourite'. This, of course, was before he became General Manager of the 'high-sounding' Great Central.

Whatever the source, the London & Southampton was undoubtedly the target of some ill-natured sniping at that period. One critic claimed that the line would be useful only for conveying prawns from Southampton and parsons from Winchester, and this 'Prawns and Parsons' label stuck in the public memory.

The management was now contemplating another branch. It was to run from Bishopstoke (now Eastleigh) on the main line, to Gosport on the shores of Portsmouth Harbour; a route had been surveyed by Giles. In 1836 Giles took up his duties with the Southampton Docks Company. The timing was unfortunate, for progress with building the railway had been slow and exposed

Left:
**A view showing the earthworks at Weybridge Cutting. It was of this that George Stephenson had foretold that 'The whole wealth and strength of the company will be forever buried in the cutting through St George's Hill at Weybridge'.**

Below left:
**Weybridge viaduct under construction. The land in the foreground became the famous Brooklands racetrack and later the Vickers aircraft factory.**

him to the charge that he was devoting too much time to his other activities. Coming under pressure, he chose to resign. The company then appointed Joseph Locke to succeed him. Locke was something of a catch; his reputation as an engineer was second only to that of Robert Stephenson and he was fresh from his work on the Grand Junction Railway which was putting the last link in the chain of rail communication between London and the North-West.

Locke abandoned the methods of working followed by Giles, who had appointed a number of small contractors to build different sections of the line. They had been paid on the basis of a certain sum per cubic yard of embankment or cutting constructed. Often finishing the easier portions of their sections first, they demanded a higher rate for the difficult ones. Others simply had not the money to carry on. Work was delayed by the negotiations and at worst stopped altogether. Locke put the unfinished work in the hands of one man, the well known contractor Thomas Brassey, and events were soon moving towards completion of the first section of line from the London terminus at Nine Elms.

The management was still beset with anxieties, however, for it was being suggested that the railway would not carry enough traffic to pay a dividend. Most of the traffic would come from the roads, and it would be useful to know the current state of the road transport business to estimate how much the railway could expect. The information the directors needed came from an unexpected quarter. W. J. Chaplin of the coaching firm Chaplin & Horne was a realist who foresaw the eclipse of his company's business. He came into the railway camp and using his intimate knowledge of the road transport industry produced a well-founded and encouraging estimate of railway expenditure and revenue which reassured the directors. He also persuaded his partner that they should sell all their stock and equipment except what could be used to operate railway feeder services. His next move was to leave for Switzerland where for some weeks he remained aloof from all business contacts and inquisitive journalists. On his return, having clearly employed his time in making momentous decisions, he invested a large sum in the London & Southampton Railway Company. In due course he became its Chairman.

By 12 May 1838 the railway was ready for the directors and other notables to travel from the London terminus at Nine Elms to Woking Common and back, an excursion followed by the banquet and speeches customary on such

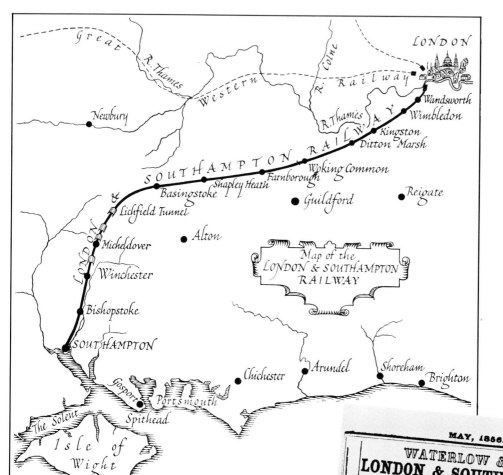

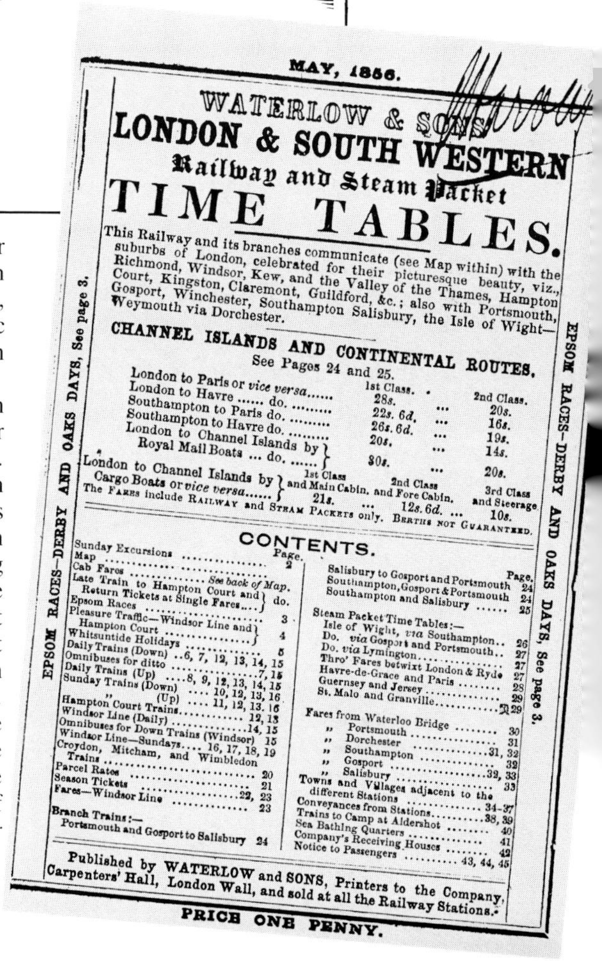

Map of the
LONDON & SOUTHAMPTON
RAILWAY

occasions. A week later there was another trip for favoured passengers, who lunched at Woking in tents erected on the common for the occasion, watched by an admiring crowd. Public traffic between Nine Elms and Woking Common began without ceremony on 21 May.

The London terminus at Nine Elms was on marshy ground on the south bank of the River Thames, dotted with bushes and windmills. Omnibuses to and from the City connected with the trains, or passengers could travel by steamers which called at a number of places between London Bridge and Nine Elms, where the landing place was close to the station. On the railway there were intermediate stations en route to Woking at Wandsworth (a little to the west of the present Clapham Junction), Wimbledon, Kingston, Ditton Marsh (later Esher), Walton and Weybridge. Kingston station was at the point where the line passed under the Ewell road and was built on the London side of the bridge. The arrival of the railway in this area sparked off a flurry of housebuilding. Early in 1840 the *Observer*

MAY, 1856.

WATERLOW & SONS
LONDON & SOUTH WESTERN
Railway and Steam Packet
TIME TABLES.

This Railway and its branches communicate (see Map within) with the suburbs of London, celebrated for their picturesque beauty, viz., Richmond, Windsor, Kew, and the Valley of the Thames, Hampton Court, Kingston, Claremont, Guildford, &c.; also with Portsmouth, Gosport, Winchester, Southampton Salisbury, the Isle of Wight—Weymouth via Dorchester.

**CHANNEL ISLANDS AND CONTINENTAL ROUTES.**
See Pages 24 and 25.

|  | 1st Class. | 2nd Class. |
|---|---|---|
| London to Paris or *vice versa* ...... | 28s. | 20s. |
| London to Havre ...... do. | | |
| Southampton to Paris do. ......... | 22s. 6d. | 16s. |
| Southampton to Havre do. | 26s. 6d. | 19s. |
| London to Channel Islands by } do. | 20s. | 14s. |
| Royal Mail Boats ... do. | 30s. | 20s. |

| | 1st Class | 2nd Class and Main Cabin. | 3rd Class and Fore Cabin. |
|---|---|---|---|
| London to Channel Islands by } Cargo Boats or *vice versa* ...... | 21s. | 12s. 6d. | 10s. |

The FARES include RAILWAY and STEAM PACKETS only. BERTHS NOT GUARANTEED.

**CONTENTS.**

| | Page. |
|---|---|
| Sunday Excursions ...... | 2 |
| Map ...... | See back of Map. |
| Cab Fares ...... | |
| Late Train to Hampton Court and } do. | |
| Return Tickets at Single Fare } | |
| Epsom Races ...... | |
| Pleasure Traffic—Windsor Line and } | 3 |
| Hampton Court ...... } | |
| Whitsuntide Holidays ...... | 4 |
| Daily Trains (Down) ...6, 7, 12, 13, 14, 15 | 5 |
| Omnibuses for ditto ...... | |
| Daily Trains (Up) ...... 7, 18 | |
| Sunday Trains (Down) ...8, 9, 12, 13, 14, 15 | |
| " (Up) ... 10, 12, 13, 16 | |
| Hampton Court Trains ... 11, 12, 13, 16 | |
| Windsor Line (Daily) ...... 12, 13 | |
| Windsor Line—Sundays (Windsor) 15 | |
| Omnibuses for Down Trains (Windsor) 14, 15 | |
| Croydon, Mitcham, and Wimbledon } 16, 17, 18, 19 | |
| Trains ...... } | |
| Parcel Rates ...... | 20 |
| Season Tickets ...... | 21 |
| Fares—Windsor Line ...... 22, 23 | |
| Branch Trains:— | |
| Portsmouth and Gosport to Salisbury 24 | |

| | Page. |
|---|---|
| Salisbury to Gosport and Portsmouth 24 | |
| Southampton, Gosport & Portsmouth 24 | |
| Southampton and Salisbury ...... 25 | |
| Steam Packet Time Tables:— | |
| Isle of Wight, *via* Southampton.. 26 | |
| Do. *via* Gosport and Portsmouth.. 27 | |
| Do. *via* Lymington ...... 27 | |
| Thro' Fares betwixt London & Ryde 27 | |
| Havre-de-Grace and Paris ...... 28 | |
| Guernsey and Jersey ...... 28 | |
| St. Malo and Granville ...... 29 | |
| Fares from Waterloo Bridge :— | |
| " Portsmouth ...... 30 | |
| " Dorchester ...... 31 | |
| " Southampton ...... 31, 32 | |
| " Gosport ...... 32 | |
| " Salisbury ...... 32, 33 | |
| Towns and Villages adjacent to the | |
| different Stations ...... 33 | |
| Conveyances from Stations .. 34–37 | |
| Trains to Camp at Aldershot ... 38, 39 | |
| Sea Bathing Quarters ...... 40 | |
| Company's Receiving Houses ... 41 | |
| Notice to Passengers ...... 42 | |
| " ...... 43, 44, 45 | |

Published by WATERLOW and SONS, Printers to the Company, Carpenters' Hall, London Wall, and sold at all the Railway Stations.

**PRICE ONE PENNY.**

*Vertical text left margin:* EPSOM RACES—DERBY AND OAKS DAYS. See page 3.

*Vertical text right margin:* EPSOM RACES—DERBY AND OAKS DAYS, See page 3.

newspaper commented: 'a completely new town is in the course of formation between the old corporation of Kingston-upon-Thames (Surrey) and the South Western Railway, and already nearly 200 new houses, snug and aristocratic villas, are finished, or in the course of finishing'. This was the nucleus of the Surbiton of today. The station was moved further west, to its present site, in 1845 but it was still called Kingston until the branch from Twickenham to the present Kingston station was opened on 1 July 1863.

On 24 September 1838 the railway was extended from Woking Common to Shapley Heath (Winchfield), with an intermediate station at Farnborough. Shapley Heath became a busy coaching centre with coaches serving the South-West and West of England calling there for the convenience of railway travellers. The line onwards to Basingstoke was opened on 10 July 1839, coinciding with the opening from Southampton to Winchester. Travellers were conveyed by coach between the two railheads. At last, on 11 May 1840, the railway was opened throughout between London and Southampton. The first down train was greeted with a salute of 21 guns on arrival, but the locomotive of the first up train burst a boiler tube and steamed into Nine Elms 1½hr late, probably upsetting the plans for its reception. Elsewhere along the route 'cold collations' and the roasting of an ox entertained those who had laboured to build the line.

The railway was engineered with easy gradients and generally gentle curvature. This had been achieved at the expense of some heavy earthworks; in fact George Stephenson had foretold that 'the whole wealth and strength of the company will be forever buried in the cutting through St George's Hill at Weybridge'. Personal feelings must be suspected here, for the engineer Giles had given evidence against the Liverpool & Manchester Bill, saying that no engineer in his senses would go through Chat Moss if he wanted to make a railway from Liverpool to Manchester.

Heavy chalk cuttings and several short tunnels were necessary in the 17 miles between Bishopstoke and the summit of the line at Litchfield tunnel, which was 400ft higher in elevation than the termini at Southampton and London. Much of the route from Nine Elms was on embankment but the heaviest work of this kind was on the descent from Micheldever towards Winchester, where a gradient of 1 in 250 was maintained. It continued to impress travellers for many years and a guidebook of 1880 mentioned a 'very steep embankment 100ft above the level of the surrounding meadows' among the memorable features of the journey. The management was sanguine over the prospects for the new line, and in the report for the first half of 1837 had observed

that 'It is highly worthy of remark that the circumstances of this railway having one of its termini at the water's edge in Southampton harbour and the other at a wharf on the banks of the Thames, affords every convenience which Nature and Art combined can give . . .'.

Early travellers may have wished there had been more evidence of 'Art' in the design of the carriages. In the First Class the compartments were so narrow that the knees of those sitting opposite to each other were in close and uncomfortable contact. In the Second Class, space was equally restricted and the seats were bare boards while the carriages were open to the weather on each side. Third Class travellers rode at first in open flat trucks with seats attached to a movable framework. When the truck was required for goods transport the framework could be removed. These rudimentary vehicles were attached to goods trains until 1842 when Third Class carriages were attached to the first morning trains, a measure which the Chairman said would 'not only give the industrious poor a greater chance of security but also encouragement for early rising'.

In 1845 Parliament decreed a better deal. Improved Third Class carriages with a narrow ventilation opening that could be closed by curtains when required, and glazed lights in the roof, were then introduced. There was seating for 30 passengers. The glazed lights were much admired at a time when few railways fitted glass in any part of their Third Class coaches, and the South Western Third Class accommodation was described as the best in the country.

There were hectic scenes at the Nine Elms terminus on Derby Day in 1838. The railway had advertised special trains to Kingston for racegoers on their way to Epsom Downs. In fact, the opening of the line had been hastened in anticipation of this traffic. When Derby Day arrived, railway officials were astonished to find a crowd estimated at 5,000 waiting for them to open up the station. Some trains were got away but the crowds kept on thronging in. The ticket clerks were overwhelmed and an impatient mob scrambled over the counter, leapt through the windows and invaded a train that had been chartered by a private party. The police were called to clear the station and at noon a notice was posted announcing that no more trains would run. Undeterred by this experience, the company advertised trains to Woking for Ascot races the following week and this time appear to have coped successfully, giving a preview of the years ahead when race traffic to the courses to the southwest of London would be handled competently and the railway would earn the gratitude of the racegoing public.

*Continued on page 13*

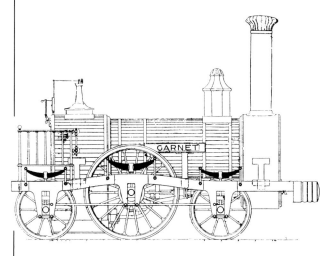

Above:
**The earliest LSWR locomotive known to have been photographed is No 8 *Vesta*, built by Sharp, Roberts and Company in 1838.**

Left:
**As with most of the pioneer railways, early locomotives were mostly 2-2-0s, 2-2-2s or 2-4-0s. *Garnet* was one of five 2-2-2 engines built for the London & Southampton Railway by the London firm of George and John Rennie in June 1838. However, they never proved very popular and were sent for complete reconstruction by Fairbairns in 1841.**

Below:
**The driver and fireman stand on the exposed footplate of this 'Mazeppa' class 2-2-2 No 57 *Meteor*. She was one of 10 six-wheeled singles built at Nine Elms in 1846-47. These engines had a trouble-free life and were renowned for their fast running.** The Bucknall Collection/Ian Allan Library

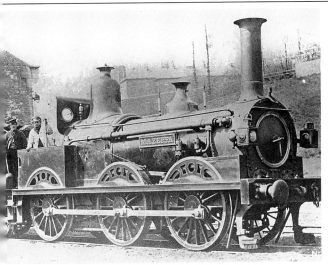

Left:
**The 'Lion' class was the first six-coupled type designed by Joseph Beattie at Nine Elms in 1863. No 53 *Mazeppa* was based at Salisbury and worked on main line goods duties.** Ian Allan Library

Below:
**No 84 *Styx*, one of Beattie's 'Falcon' class express engines, built in 1864, was one of many 2-4-0 locomotives, and was one of a pair responsible for working the fast express trains between Waterloo, Salisbury and Yeovil. She is seen here at Bournemouth in 1889.** L&GRP (21870)

Bottom:
**This unnamed 'Vesuvius' class 2-4-0 No 294 was built at Nine Elms in 1873. She is seen here in her latter days fitted with an Adams chimney.** The Bucknall Collection/Ian Allan Library

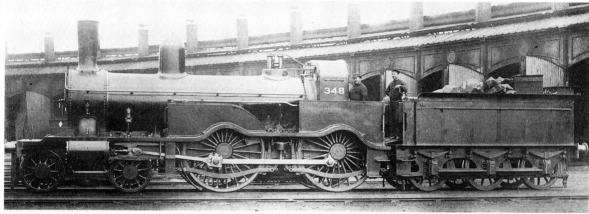

Top:
**One of the better known of Beattie's engines were the 7ft 2-4-0s. No 75 *Fireking* entered service in 1864 and was the second in the series built between 1859 and 1868. She is seen in this view at Exeter.** L&GRP (30724)

Above:
**The first of 20 4-4-0s of the '348' class built for the LSWR, No 348, was designed by Joseph Beattie's son W. G. Beattie and built by Sharp Stewart in**

**1876. These engines were found to be very unsatisfactory and were rebuilt by Adams in 1888.** Ian Allan Library

Below:
**The graceful looks of No 348 after rebuilding were typical of all locomotives designed by William Adams. However, the reconstruction did not greatly improve their performance and the scheme was discontinued in 1890, with only eight of the class having been affected.** Ian Allan Library

*Continued from page 9*

Traffic was worked at first with four-wheel locomotives built by outside firms, but the change to 2-2-2 designs soon followed. Joseph Woods was Locomotive Superintendent until succeeded by J. V. Gooch, brother of Daniel Gooch, on 1 January 1841. Under Gooch the railway began building its own locomotives at Nine Elms in 1843, a practice which was to continue and be made memorable by such famous names as Beattie, Adams and Drummond, until locomotive manufacture was moved to Eastleigh in 1909. The original works were on the north side of the present main line, adjacent to the running lines into the Nine Elms terminus. In 1865 they were moved to a more commodious site on the south side together with a new locomotive depot.

In spite of omnibuses and Thames steamers, Nine Elms was not a convenient terminus. A move closer to the centre of things was desirable and various schemes were considered. A report of one directors' meeting stated that 'the project for a central railway terminus on the north bank of the Thames near Charing Cross is deemed a subject worthy of mature consideration'. But the railway remained south of the river. In 1847 it acquired the Richmond & West End Railway which in 1845 had been given powers to build a line from Richmond to join the South Western at the present Clapham Junction and to run from there to Nine Elms, its line continuing to a terminus at Waterloo Bridge. The railway was opened from Richmond to Clapham Junction on 27 July 1846 and its trains used the existing tracks onwards to Nine Elms. The South Western built the Nine Elms-Waterloo Bridge section, adding two tracks for the Richmond trains from Clapham Junction to the new terminus. In 1847 a company was formed to build an extension from Richmond to Windsor and the extra lines laid for the Richmond trains accordingly became known as the Windsor Lines.

The extension from Nine Elms to Waterloo, known as the Metropolitan Extension, was opened on 11 July 1848. It was 1¾ miles in length and was carried on 290 arches, with six bridges where roads passed under the line. The new terminus, at first called Waterloo Bridge, had four platform lines and two middle roads. Land was bought for a continuation to London Bridge but this never materialised. In 1864, however, when the South Eastern Railway was extended from London Bridge to Charing Cross, one of the middle roads was extended across the station concourse to join the South Eastern at Waterloo Junction (now Waterloo East). For a few months in 1865 a train service between Euston and London Bridge via the West London line used the connection but for the rest of its existence it carried only occasional special workings or vans being exchanged between the two lines. Normally it was bridged by a section of movable platform level with the rest of the concourse, the track being slightly sunk. Waterloo grew in a haphazard manner that aroused much criticism from the travelling public and was ridiculed by Jerome K. Jerome in *Three Men in a Boat*. When it was rebuilt in 1922 the whole layout was rationalised and the connection to Waterloo Junction was removed.

Apart from this episode London Bridge remained out of reach. When an extension from Waterloo eventually crossed the Thames to the City it did so in a tube tunnel. The Waterloo & City electric underground railway opened its line from Waterloo to the Bank on 8 August 1898. It was built by an independent company supported by the South Western, which took the line over in 1907. The line was 1 mile 46ch long, with no intermediate station. Its rolling stock of motor-coaches and trailers lived underground like pit ponies, emerging only for servicing when they were lifted from the depths by a hoist in the yard at Waterloo. This procedure has continued. Regular users call the line the 'Drain'. For the rest it is usually 'out of sight, out of mind' and like most drains one only becomes aware of it when something goes wrong and a notice in the main concourse at Waterloo warns of an interruption of

Left:
**Woking Common in 1838, a journey of 23 miles was completed in just under 1hr. The station itself was 1½ miles from the village of (Old) Woking, but after the arrival of the L&SR a new town soon developed, to the north of the railway.**

# LONDON AND SOUTH WESTERN
# RAILWAY
# On and after November 9th.

## HOURS OF DEPARTURE, AND TIME TABLE.

### Down Trains.

| LEAVE STATIONS. | mixed. | stopping. | stopping. | Fast Train. | Goods. | stopping. | stopping. | mixed. | stopping. | stopping. | stopping. | Fast Mail. | Goods. |
|---|---|---|---|---|---|---|---|---|---|---|---|---|---|
| | h. m. | h. m. | h. m. | h. m. | h. m. | h. m. | h. m. | h. m. | h. m. | h. m. | h. m. | h. m. | h. m. |
| NINE ELMS .... | 7. 0 | 9. 0 | 9.30 | 11.0 | 12. 0 | 12. 0 | 1. 0 | .... | 4. 0 | 5. 0 | 6. 0 | 8.30 | 8.45 |
| Wandsworth .. | .... | 9. 8 | 9.38 | .... | .... | 12. 8 | 1. 8 | .... | 4. 8 | 5. 8 | 6. 8 | .... | .... |
| Wimbledon.... | .... | 9.18 | 9.48 | .... | .... | 12.18 | 1.18 | .... | 4.18 | 5.18 | 6.18 | .... | .... |
| Kingston...... | .... | 9.32 | 10. 2 | .... | 12.43 | 12.32 | 1.32 | .... | 4.32 | 5.32 | 6.32 | 8.52 | 9.28 |
| Esher ........ | .... | 9.41 | 10.11 | .... | 12.57 | 12.41 | 1.41 | .... | 4.41 | 5.41 | 6.41 | .... | 9.42 |
| Walton ...... | .... | 9.50 | 10.20 | .... | 1.12 | 12.50 | 1.50 | .... | 4.50 | 5.50 | 6.50 | .... | 9.57 |
| Weybridge .... | .... | 9.58 | 10.30 | .... | 1.26 | 1. 0 | 1.58 | .... | 5. 0 | 5.58 | 7. 0 | 9. 9 | 10.11 |
| Woking ...... | 7.57 | 10.15 | .... | 11.46 | 1.54 | .... | 2.15 | .... | .... | 6.16 | 7.15 | 9.24 | 10.39 |
| Farnborough .. | 8.27 | 10.45 | .... | 12.12 | 2.37 | .... | 2.45 | .... | .... | 6.45 | .... | 9.51 | 11.22 |
| Winchfield .... | 8.46 | 11. 4 | .... | 12.29 | 3. 9 | .... | 3. 4 | .... | .... | 7. 4 | .... | 10. 8 | 11.54 |
| Basingstoke .. | 9. 7 | 11.25 | .... | 12.50 | 3.48 | .... | 3.25 | .... | .... | 7.25 | .... | 10.29 | 12.33 |
| Andover Road | 9.39 | 11.57 | .... | 1.17 | 4.35 | .... | 3.57 | .... | .... | 7.57 | .... | 10.57 | 1.20 |
| Winchester .. | 10. 0 | 12.18 | .... | 1.34 | 5.10 | .... | 4.18 | .... | .... | 8.18 | .... | 11.14 | 1.55 |
| SOUTHAMPTON. | 10.30 | 12.48 | .... | 2. 0 | 6. 0 | .... | 4.48 | .... | .... | 8.48 | .... | 11.40 | 2.45 |

### Up Trains to London.

| LEAVE STATIONS. | Mail. | stopping. | stopping. | stopping. | stopping. | Goods. | Fast Train. | stopping. | stopping. | mixed. | stopping. | stopping. | Goods. |
|---|---|---|---|---|---|---|---|---|---|---|---|---|---|
| | h. m. | h. m. | h. m. | h. m. | h. m. | h. m. | h. m. | h. m. | h. m. | h. m. | h. m. | h. m. | h. m. |
| SOUTHAMPTON. | 2. 0 | .... | 6. 0 | .... | 8.30 | 10. 0 | 11. 0 | .... | 1.30 | .... | .... | 6. 0 | 8. 0 |
| Winchester .. | 2.29 | .... | 6.34 | .... | 9. 4 | 10.57 | 11.29 | .... | 2. 4 | .... | .... | 6.34 | 8.57 |
| Andover Road | 2.53 | .... | 7. 0 | .... | 9.30 | 11.37 | 11.53 | .... | 2.30 | .... | .... | 7. 0 | 9.37 |
| Basingstoke .. | 3.13 | .... | 7.23 | .... | 9.53 | 12.23 | 12.13 | .... | 2.53 | .... | .... | 7.23 | 10.23 |
| Winchfield .... | 3.32 | .... | 7.46 | .... | 10.16 | 12.59 | 12.32 | .... | 3.16 | .... | .... | 7.46 | 10.59 |
| Farnborough .. | 3.49 | .... | 8. 5 | .... | 10.35 | 1.29 | 12.49 | .... | 3.35 | .... | .... | 8. 5 | 11.29 |
| Woking ...... | 4. 7 | 7.45 | 8.27 | .... | 10.57 | 2. 5 | 1. 7 | .... | 3.57 | .... | .... | 8.27 | 12. 5 |
| Weybridge .... | 4.23 | 7.57 | 8.44 | 10.45 | 11.14 | 2.33 | .... | 2. 0 | 4.16 | .... | 7. 0 | 8.44 | 12.33 |
| Walton ...... | .... | 8. 5 | 8.51 | 10.50 | 11.22 | 2.46 | .... | 2. 5 | 4.22 | .... | 7. 8 | 8.53 | 12.46 |
| Esher ........ | .... | 8.13 | 9. 0 | 10.58 | 11.30 | 3. 0 | .... | 2.13 | 4.30 | .... | 7.13 | 9. 0 | 1. 0 |
| Kingston...... | 4.41 | 8.25 | 9.10 | 11.10 | 11.40 | 3.14 | .... | 2.25 | 4.40 | .... | 7.25 | 9.10 | 1.14 |
| Wimbledon.... | .... | 8.39 | 9.26 | 11.24 | 11.56 | .... | .... | 2.39 | 4.56 | .... | 7.39 | 9.26 | .... |
| Wandsworth .. | .... | 8.50 | 9.37 | 11.35 | 12. 7 | .... | .... | 2.50 | 5. 7 | .... | 7.50 | 9.37 | .... |
| NINE ELMS .... | 5. 4 | 9. 0 | 9.46 | 11.45 | 12.16 | 4. 0 | 2. 0 | 3. 0 | 5.16 | 6. 0 | 8. 0 | 9.46 | 2. 0 |

## ON SUNDAYS.

### Down Trains.

| LEAVE STATIONS. | stop. | stop. | stop. | stop. | stop. | stop. | Mail. |
|---|---|---|---|---|---|---|---|
| | h. m. | h. m. | h. m. | h. m. | h. m. | h. m. | h. m. |
| NINE ELMS ... | 9 0 | 10 0 | 10 30 | 2 0 | 5 0 | 7 30 | 8 30 |
| Wandsworth .. | 9 8 | 10 8 | 10 38 | 2 8 | 5 8 | 7 38 | .... |
| Wimbledon.... | 9 18 | 10 18 | 10 48 | 2 18 | 5 18 | 7 48 | .... |
| Kingston...... | 9 32 | 10 32 | 11 2 | 2 32 | 5 32 | 8 2 | 8 52 |
| Esher ........ | 9 41 | 10 41 | 11 11 | 2 41 | 5 41 | 8 11 | .... |
| Walton ...... | 9 50 | 10 50 | 11 20 | 2 50 | 5 50 | 8 20 | .... |
| Weybridge .... | 9 58 | 10 58 | 11 28 | 2 58 | 5 58 | 8 28 | 9 9 |
| Woking ...... | 10 15 | 11 15 | 11 45 | 3 15 | 6 15 | 8 45 | 9 24 |
| Farnboro' .... | .... | 11 45 | .... | .... | 6 45 | .... | 9 51 |
| Winchfield .... | .... | 12 4 | .... | .... | 7 4 | .... | 10 8 |
| Basingstoke .. | .... | 12 25 | .... | .... | 7 25 | .... | 10 29 |
| Andover Road | .... | 12 57 | .... | .... | 7 57 | .... | 10 57 |
| Winchester .. | .... | 1 18 | .... | .... | 8 18 | .... | 11 14 |
| SOUTHAMPTON. | .... | 1 48 | .... | .... | 8 48 | .... | 11 40 |

### Up Trains to London.

| LEAVE STATIONS. | Mail. | stop. | stop. | stop. | stop. | stop. | stop. |
|---|---|---|---|---|---|---|---|
| | h. m. | h. m. | h. m. | h. m. | h. m. | h. m. | h. m. |
| SOUTHAMPTON | 2 0 | .... | 10 0 | .... | 5 0 | .... | .... |
| Winchester .. | 2 29 | .... | 10 34 | .... | 5 34 | .... | .... |
| Andover Road | 2 53 | .... | 11 0 | .... | 6 0 | .... | .... |
| Basingstoke .. | 3 13 | .... | 11 23 | .... | 6 23 | .... | .... |
| Winchfield .... | 3 32 | .... | 11 46 | .... | 6 46 | .... | .... |
| Farnboro' .... | 3 49 | .... | 12 5 | .... | 7 5 | .... | .... |
| Woking ...... | 4 7 | 8 0 | 12 27 | 11 0 | 7 27 | 6 0 | 8 0 |
| Weybridge .... | 4 23 | 8 12 | 12 44 | 11 12 | 7 44 | 6 12 | 8 12 |
| Walton ...... | .... | 8 20 | 12 52 | 11 20 | 7 52 | 6 20 | 8 20 |
| Esher ........ | .... | 8 28 | 1 0 | 11 28 | 8 0 | 6 28 | 8 28 |
| Kingston...... | 4 41 | 8 40 | 1 10 | 11 40 | 8 10 | 6 40 | 8 40 |
| Wimbledon.... | .... | 8 54 | 1 26 | 11 54 | 8 26 | 6 54 | 8 54 |
| Wandsworth | .... | 9 5 | 1 37 | 12 5 | 8 37 | 7 5 | 9 5 |
| NINE ELMS .... | 5 4 | 9 15 | 1 46 | 12 15 | 8 46 | 7 15 | 9 15 |

Goods' Trains as on other Days.

☞ London Time will be observed, and the Doors of the Stations closed at the Times given above.

16th August, 1840     *Smith and Ebbs, Printers, Tower-hill, London.*

service. But historically the 'Drain' deserves more respect. It was the second electric underground railway in London, preceded only by the City & South London, opened in 1890. And it was the first London underground with motorcoach trains. Both the City & South London and the Central London in 1900 hauled their trains with electric locomotives at first.

At Southampton the Docks company began to develop the port by laying the foundation stone of the first deep water dock in 1838. The first ships to use it were two P&O vessels in August 1848, one of them discharging passengers and cargo direct into a train at the dockside. This preceded the public opening on 1 July 1843 when the P&O steamship *Pacha* arrived from Gibraltar. Traffic grew over the years and further docks were built, but by the end of the century the cost of necessary new works had become greater than the Docks company could meet from its own resources. At first a loan was obtained from the railway, but when further expenditure was required negotiations were begun for the railway to take over the docks itself. The purchase was approved by Parliament and took effect from 1 November 1892.

Left:
**The railway was opened throughout to Southampton on 11 May 1840, a distance of 77 miles and was covered in a little over 3hr, but by 1847 this had been cut to under 2hr.**

Below:
**An old woodcut showing an early scene on the L&SR at Wandsworth Cutting. The engine is a Sharp 2-2-2, a type supplied to a number of railway companies at that time.**

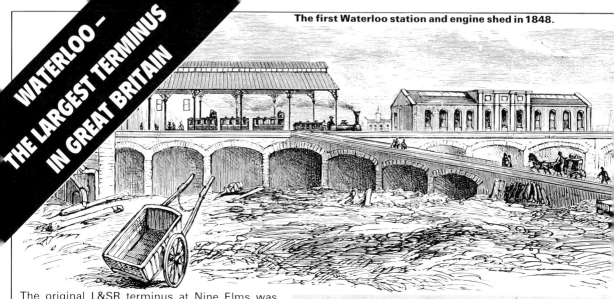

The first Waterloo station and engine shed in 1848.

The original L&SR terminus at Nine Elms was considered rather remote from Central London, so it was decided to seek permission to build a new station closer to the City. In 1844 an Act was passed for the 'Metropolitan Extension' from Nine Elms to a point near Waterloo Bridge. Work began in July 1846, at a time when London was confined mainly to the north of the River Thames. Londoners considered the Surrey side as a resort for their recreation, with its three gardens, at Vauxhall, Belvedere and Cupers. It was said that the new building operations displaced nothing of any value, since the terminus was to be erected on ground occupied by hay-stolls, cow yards, dung heaps and other nuisances. A new four-track extension was to be built from Nine Elms, raised above the marshy ground along a 1.75-mile viaduct. Four tracks were considered enough to cope with the traffic of the day, and any growth in the foreseeable future.

East of Vauxhall the line twisted and curved, first to avoid Vauxhall Gardens, which continued to flourish until 1859, then to miss the old gas-works and finally to avoid the grounds of Lambeth Palace. Like the approach road, the station was built entirely on arches. The architect was Sir William Tite, the engineer Joseph Locke and the contractors were Lee & Son of Chiswell Street. There were three platforms each 300ft long, which were later extended to 600ft. Offices ran parallel with the platforms. On each side of the station was a cab road and at the west end there was an engine shed. The official date of opening was 11 July 1848, but it was two days later before the first train arrived, the honour went to the 1.05am up train from Southampton, arriving at Waterloo at 4.30am, headed by the locomotive *Hornet* pulling seven coaches. From this date Nine Elms became a locomotive depot and workshop.

At first the new station was referred to as either York Road, the road-side station near Waterloo, Waterloo Bridge or Waterloo. The latter two

names were used indiscriminately until 1886, when Waterloo Bridge appeared for the last time. By 1850 the traffic into and out of Waterloo had doubled and in 1862 a new North station was opened for Windsor line trains, increasing the number of platforms to seven. In 1864 a line was extended over the concourse, to join the South Eastern Railway's new extension from London Bridge to Charing Cross, adjacent to Waterloo Junction. In 1879 a separate South station was opened to handle suburban trains to and from the Epsom, Hampton Court and Shepperton branches. Further platforms had been added to

Right:
**The exterior of the Old Buildings prior to 1911. The bridge on the left carried the line which linked the LSWR to the SECR. Today this is now a footbridge, carrying passengers between the main station and Waterloo East.**

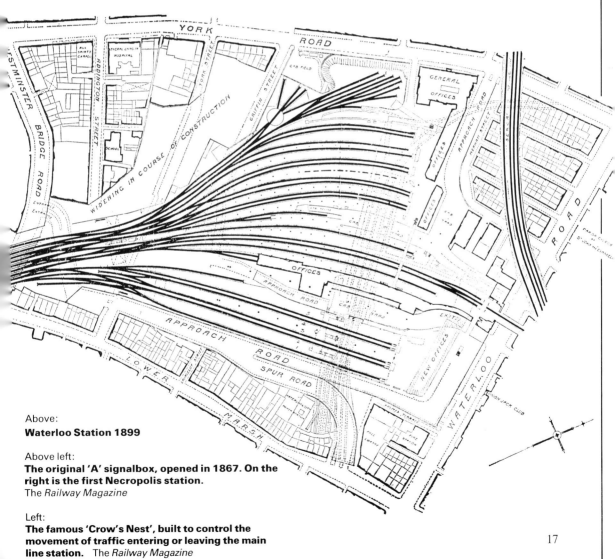

Above:
**Waterloo Station 1899**

Above left:
**The original 'A' signalbox, opened in 1867. On the right is the first Necropolis station.**
The *Railway Magazine*

Left:
**The famous 'Crow's Nest', built to control the movement of traffic entering or leaving the main line station.** The *Railway Magazine*

17

**Waterloo Station 1922**

YORK ROAD

TO CHARING STATION

WESTMINSTER BRIDGE ROAD

SIGNAL BOX

END OF MAIN PLATFORM

PLATFORM ROOF

STATION OFFICES

CAB ROAD

21
20 19
18 17
16
15
14 13
12
11
10 9
8 7
6 5
4 3
2 1

HOIST

EXITS

EXITS

EXIT

CONCOURSE

CONCOURSE

GENERAL OFFICES

APPROACH ROAD

WATERLOO (EASTERN SECT.)

ROAD

CAB ROAD

WATERLOO

TO WATERLOO (EASTERN SE...

TO WATERLOO (EASTERN SE...

NEWS THEATRE (OVERHEAD)

SUB STATION

APPROACH ROAD

LOWER MARSH

### KEY TO RUNNING LINES

| | |
|---|---|
| W . . Up Windsor | MT . . Up Main Through |
| WT . . Down Windsor Through | MT . . Down Main Through |
| WL . . Down Windsor Local | ML . . Up Main Local |
| MR . . Up Main Through Relief | ML . . Down Main Local |

the North station and by 1885 the total number of platforms reached 14, with 18 lines, handling a total of 500 trains daily.

To begin with there was only one signal outside the station yard, operated by a man standing on the ground. For many years there was a signalbox known as the 'Crow's Nest', wedged under the gable roof over the main line platforms, from where a signalman controlled traffic entering or leaving them. The first 'A' box opened in 1867, straddling the four tracks, and was equipped with 47 levers. It survived until 1874 when a new 'A' box replaced the old one, at first containing 109 levers. By 1885 this was in turn increased to 180 levers and was said to be the largest signalbox in England. Three years later Waterloo 'A' box was again reconstructed and equipped with 229 levers. Meanwhile, work had commenced on widening the approaches outside the station, increasing the number of running lines from four to six.

By now the growth of the station was far from convenient. The South station was a kind of annexe, reached by a covered bridge, and was separated from the North station by the Central station, which handled all the main line traffic. At the close of the 19th century, the total traffic dealt with at Waterloo had reached 700 trains per day, carrying 100,000 passengers. In 1899 the Board of Directors realised that nothing short of complete reconstruction would solve the problem, and it was decided to obtain powers to build an entirely new station with 23 platforms. By 1903 the land had been prepared following extensive slum clearance and the rehousing of 1,750 displaced

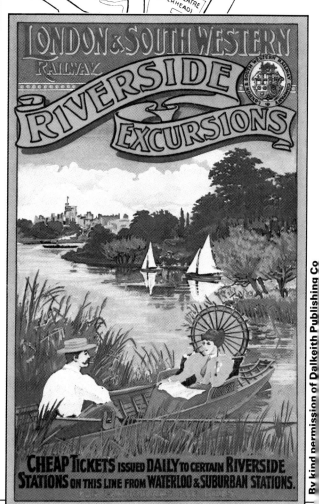

LONDON & SOUTH WESTERN RAILWAY

RIVERSIDE EXCURSIONS

CHEAP TICKETS ISSUED DAILY TO CERTAIN RIVERSIDE STATIONS ON THIS LINE FROM WATERLOO & SUBURBAN STATIONS.

By kind permission of Dalkeith Publishing Co

persons. However, it was not until 1910 that the first section opened to traffic, replacing the old South station. The original general offices had entirely disappeared by 1913, and three months later 11 platforms were in use. Progress was delayed during World War 1 — especially on the station buildings. In 1919 the escalators to the Waterloo & City line were brought into use and the famous clock was placed centrally over the concourse. The original plans had to be modified to retain the 1855 Windsor line station (Platforms 16-21) which was separated from the main station by a range of offices, known as the 'Village'; this reduced the number of platforms from the planned 23 to the present 21. The platforms ranged in length from 550ft upwards in the Windsor line station, to around 700ft on the Shepperton side, and to 860ft for the main line departure platform — No 11. Trains of 13 coaches or more were liable to block access to adjacent platforms, as well as prevent clearance of starting signals.

The final completion was marked by the opening of the Victory Arch by Queen Mary on 21 March 1922. The builders had done what was thought to be impossible, the transformation of the 'mighty maze' of the 1880s, into a magnificent and spacious terminus, with a broad concourse giving an uninterrupted view of all 21 platform entrances. All this had been done without inconvenience to the travelling public and without serious interruption to train services.

1848
WATERLOO
STATION
CENTENARY
1948

PRICE

# Portsmouth and the Isle of Wight

The London & Southampton Railway next turned its eyes towards Portsmouth. At first the railway's plans to serve Portsmouth by a branch from Bishopstoke were objected to on the grounds that the mileage from Portsmouth to London by that route would be greater than from Southampton to London, but opposition was withdrawn later on the condition that no obstacles would be placed in the way of a more direct route. There had been two proposals for such a line, one of them planning atmospheric propulsion, but neither had gained Parliamentary approval. Local patriotism was also involved, for in some quarters the idea of Portsmouth being on a branch from a railway named the London & Southampton did not go down well. Diplomatically, a clause changing the name to London & South Western Railway was inserted in the company's Bill for lines to Gosport and Portsmouth so that feelings were soothed at the same time as the railway gained a description more appropriate to its plans for expansion. The change of name took effect from 4 June 1839.

The line from Bishopstoke to Gosport was built first. Thomas Brassey was the contractor and he followed roughly the route that had been surveyed by Giles. Passenger traffic began in November 1841 but problems with the stability of the tunnel at Fareham caused the line to be closed a few days later. It was reopened on 7 February 1842.

Gosport station was about ¾ mile from the floating bridge that crossed the harbour to Portsmouth. An omnibus bridged the gap. A new pier was built in Gosport Harbour for the Isle of Wight ferry service. The floating bridge did not run at night and passengers from Portsmouth wishing to join the night mail train from Gosport station had to cross the harbour in an open boat.

When Queen Victoria began travelling regularly to Osborne House in the Isle of Wight, the down track in Gosport station was extended for 600yd to a new 'Royal station' in the Royal Clarence Yard where the Queen and her retinue could embark on the Royal Yacht *Victoria and Albert*. The station was opened in September 1845. For many years the Queen visited Osborne twice yearly and these regular journeys helped to justify the title *A Royal Road* for Sam Fay's history of the London & South Western Railway.

From the opening of the Gosport branch through carriages were run to and from London. There were occasional criticisms of the time spent in shunting at Bishopstoke, particularly when passengers to Portsmouth missed the connection with the floating bridge as a result, but most travellers probably found this a minor incon-venience compared with the advantage of not having to change trains with the numerous and bulky items of luggage that often accompanied them.

Bishopstoke was becoming an important junction, A branch to Salisbury was opened to goods traffic on 27 January 1847 and to passenger services on 1 March in the same year. Also in 1847 an extension of the London Brighton & South Coast Railway (LBSCR) from Chichester reached Portsmouth, and on 1 October 1848 the London & South Western opened a line from Fareham on the Gosport branch to join the LBSCR at Portcreek Junction near Cosham — the remaining three miles to Portsmouth station becoming joint property. Some massive trains would be assembled and divided at Basingstoke in the years to come. Joseph Beattie told the Institution of Mechanical Engineers in 1854 of 'the Southampton, Portsmouth, Gosport and Salisbury trains all being joined at Basingstoke and taken in one train to London, which generally contains from 20 to 26 carriages'.

The LBSCR and LSWR routes to London, via Brighton and via Bishopstoke respectively, were both 95¼ miles in length. Demand for a more direct route continued. The so-called 'Direct' line which originally proposed an atmospheric system had dropped the idea and now won the support of the Portsmouth Corporation. A petition in its favour was submitted to Parliament and its Bill received the Royal Assent on 26 June 1846. The LSWR had reached Guildford from Woking on 1 May 1845 and was now authorised to build an extension to join the proposed line at Godalming and to run trains over it to Cosham. These powers were not exercised and the original London & Portsmouth Direct Railway Company was wound up in 1854. Meanwhile, a new scheme backed by the contractor Thomas Brassey had come on the scene. This was for a line from Godalming to Havant on the LBSCR, and it was authorised by an Act of 8 July 1853. The Act also gave power for an independent line from Havant to Hilsea on the LSWR/LBSCR joint line into Portsmouth.

Obviously the best prospect for the railway was to carry LSWR traffic, which would be given a much shorter route to Portsmouth from Waterloo. In case this failed, however, powers were obtained for an extension from Godalming to join the South Eastern Railway line from Redhill at Shalford, which would have allowed a South Eastern London-Portsmouth service. These powers were never exercised and finally the 'Portsmouth Direct' from Godalming to Havant was leased by the

LSWR. It was hoped that LSWR trains would be given running powers over the LBSCR from Havant to Portcreek Junction, where they would join the joint line into Portsmouth. The LSWR would then have a route of only 74 miles from Waterloo to Portsmouth compared with 95 miles by the Brighton line.

The LBSCR objected strongly but the South Western determined to enforce what it saw as its rights by sending a goods train down the line on 28 December 1858. At Havant its progress was blocked by a LBSCR engine and a part of the junction points had been removed. At first there was dignified remonstrance and refusal by the principal parties, but when this led nowhere the South Western party tried to remove the obstructions by force, leading to some jostling and skirmishing among the workmen who had been brought along to clear the way or to obstruct attempts to do so. It was not as violent a scene as is suggested by the name 'Battle of Havant' by which it is remembered in railway history. At length the South Western party withdrew and the lawyers had their say on the matter in the Courts. They found in favour of the London & South Western Railway, imposing certain conditions on both railways, and the LSWR began its 'Portsmouth Direct' service on 24 January 1859. In 1861 it absorbed the Portsmouth Direct company. A cheap fares war which followed the 'battle' did little good to either combatant and in the end the Portsmouth traffic was pooled, the South Western taking two-thirds and the LBSC one-third.

The Isle of Wight traffic was of growing importance to the LSWR. Steamers plied between Clarence Pier, Southsea and the Island. At first, passengers made their own way between Portsmouth station and the pier but in 1863 a horse tramway was opened along the public roads over the intervening 1 mile 8ch. The service was primarily for railway passengers although local traffic was not excluded. Two cars coupled together — one for luggage and the other for passengers — were hauled by one or two horses according to the load and other conditions. At that time the Portsmouth fortifications prevented an extension of the railway to the harbour but when new defence works were built at Hilsea the route for the railway was clear. The extension to Portsmouth Harbour station, undertaken jointly by the LSWR and the LBSCR, was opened on 2 October 1876. A local report remarked on how the new line improved through communication with the Isle of Wight 'by getting rid of the necessity for transhipping passengers and luggage

Right:
**Drummond 'T9' 4-4-0 No 711, built by Dübs in 1899, heads a down train near Haslemere, on the Portsmouth Direct line.**
L&GRP (21343)

London & South Western Rv.
TICKET FOR PERAMBULATOR.
GO CART OR BICYCLE
Accompanied by passenger
WATERLOO (W) to
ANY STATION ON THE L.& S.W Ry
NOT EXCEEDING    25 MILES
(S.3)                   See over
Zone 25           Rate 9d
4942

from the railway at Landport to the tramcars, and from the tramcars to the unsheltered pier at Southsea, thereby adding greatly to the comfort of all, and especially of passengers in delicate health, who so frequently make this journey in the winter months'.

Portsmouth & Southsea station today stands on the site of the original Portsmouth terminus. This had been a modest single-platform affair but new buildings were erected when the harbour extension was opened. The new line left the old just east of the terminus and climbed at a gradient of 1 in 61 to an adjacent island platform in a new high level station.

Improvements in communications with the Isle of Wight were also made at Gosport. An independent company built a line 1¾ miles long from Gosport to a new pier at Stokes Bay, from which steamers sailed to the Island. The service began on 6 April 1863 with through carriages between Waterloo and Stokes Bay pier. At first the trains reversed at Gosport but in 1864 a bypass spur was brought into use. The company was soon in financial difficulties and in 1871 the South Western agreed to lease the line and eventually to purchase it. From 1875 the service was improved by taking Stokes Bay coaches non-stop from Eastleigh to the pier, giving a journey time of 2hr 45min from Waterloo to Ryde, which was 30min faster than via Portsmouth, but from the opening of Portsmouth Harbour station this advantage disappeared. Later the service was operated during the summer only. Through coaches were run to

Stokes Bay from the Midlands in the holiday season. At the end of the 1913 summer timetable the sailings to the Island were withdrawn and passenger services over the branch ended in the summer of 1914.

In the same area another private venture, the Lee-on-the-Solent Light Railway Company, opened a line 3 miles in length from Fort Brockhurst station on the South Western's Gosport branch to Lee-on-the-Solent, where a pier had been built with the intention of developing the town as a resort. The line opened on 12 May 1894 and was worked by the company until the LSWR took the operation over in 1909. The company survived until Grouping when it was absorbed into the Southern Railway. Under Southern management passenger services were withdrawn on 1 January 1931 and the line was closed completely on 28 September 1935.

Development of the South Western system south of the main line brought the railway to Alton on 8 July 1852. The Mid-Hants Railway connected Alton with Winchester on 2 October 1865, providing a useful bypass for the main line in times of trouble. A line from Alton to Fareham following the Meon Valley was opened on 1 June 1903. It shortened the distance from London to Gosport compared with the route via Eastleigh but through services were meagre and the line was mainly of local interest. Perhaps if the Stokes Bay route to the Isle of Wight had flourished, or Lee-on-the-Solent had blossomed as a resort, the Meon Valley line would have had a more important role.

# Dorchester, Weymouth and Bournemouth

After completion of the main line to Southampton and the branch from Basingstoke to Salisbury, the South Western considered plans for extension westward. The company was interested in a Southampton & Dorchester Railway being promoted by Charles Castleman, a Wimborne solicitor. Negotiations broke down when Castleman imposed conditions which were found unacceptable. One of them, couched in uncompromising language, was that the South Western should 'never henceforth project a single inch of railway to the west of Salisbury'. When he realised that this demand would not be accepted, Castleman began talks with the Great Western Railway, whose engineers had been surveying in the Weymouth and Dorchester area, and actually secured their agreement to work his line. The South Western retaliated by proposing a line from Salisbury to Weymouth as well as other schemes aimed at the area left vacant by the Great Western

line to the West in its wide sweep through Swindon and Bath. None of these proposals found favour with the Board of Trade, whose approval was necessary before a Bill could be presented to Parliament. As a compromise, however, the Southampton & Dorchester line was approved, and the South Western was authorised to lease and work it, and to exercise running powers from Dorchester to Weymouth when the Great Western built its line from Westbury to the coast.

There was some opposition in Southampton to Castleman's line and certain interests in the town urged that its terminus should be at Blechynden on what were then the western outskirts. This seems largely to have come from local traders and cab proprietors who hoped for a rich harvest from travellers making their way between Blechynden and the South Western's terminus. When the Southampton to Dorchester line was opened on 1 June 1847 the trains did in fact terminate at

Above left:
**Until 1843 Woking was known as Woking Common. Adams 'T6' 4-4-0 No 685, built at Nine Elms in 1892, approaches the down island platform with a Pullman car express for Bournemouth.**
The Bucknall Collection/
Ian Allan Library

Left:
**A down stopping train headed by Adams 'X2' 4-4-0 No 594 is seen near Winchfield. The line between Pirbright Junction and Basingstoke East was not quadrupled until July 1904.**
The Bucknall Collection/
Ian Allan Library

Rebuilt by Adams in 1890, Beattie '348' 4-4-0
No 0353 leaves Bournemouth Central with a
stopping train to Weymouth in 1902. E. W. Fry

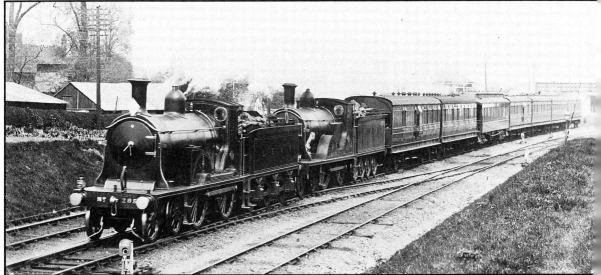

Top:
**A down freight passes Eastleigh with Drummond 'F13' No 334 in charge. To the right of the picture are the Carriage and Wagon Works and the Fareham branch.**
The Bucknall Collection/Ian Allan Library

Above:
**Before the days of corridor trains the LSWR used to include a Pullman car in the formation of some express trains on the Bournemouth line, for the use of First Class passengers paying a supplement. However, the introduction of restaurant cars brought to an end this limited use of Pullman cars on LSWR metals. In this view a down Pullman car express passes Swaythling behind an unidentified Drummond 'T9' 4-4-0 led by another 'T9', No 285 of an earlier batch built at Nine Elms in 1900.**
The Bucknall Collection/Ian Allan Library

Blechynden but this was because of problems in the tunnel through which the line continued to join the South Western. These were overcome and the line was opened through to Southampton Junction on 29 July, enabling the Dorchester trains to use the South Western's terminus. For some years through trains between London and Dorchester had to reverse at Southampton but a curve to allow through running was opened in 1858 and Blechynden was renamed Southampton West. The sharp curvature on this short connection imposed a speed limit of 15mph which was not relaxed until 1980 when it was raised to 25mph.

Castleman's railway to Dorchester wound a sinuous way westward which earned it the name of 'Castleman's Corkscrew' or the 'Watersnake'. This was partly to meet the insistence of the Woods and Forests Commissioners that it should not pass

Left:
**The short-lived Meyrick Park Halt, situated between Bournemouth Central and West, lasted in the timetable for just over 11 years from May 1906 until October 1917. In this view Drummond 'T14' 4-6-0 No 446 heads a four-coach passenger train.**
L&GRP (12960)

through the wooded areas of the New Forest; it was also designed to serve as many sizeable places as possible. Bournemouth was then only a small winter health resort and there seemed to be more potential traffic from Ringwood and Wimborne. The line therefore curved further inland after Brockenhurst and did not touch the coast until Poole Harbour, Here there was a station called Poole Junction and a branch to Poole (the name was changed later to Hamworthy).

Between Brockenhurst and Ringwood there was a station called Christchurch Road on the main road from Southampton to the coast. A coach ran from the station to Christchurch, about 7 miles away. The traveller to Bournemouth could join another coach there and jog along over the remaining 5 miles to the resort.

Various proposals for a railway to Christchurch ran into difficulties and it was not until 13 November 1862 that a single-track branch was opened from Ringwood. An extension to Bourne-

mouth was authorised in the following year but the economy was in the doldrums and the line was not opened until 14 March 1870. The terminus was called Bournemouth East and it gave Bournemouth its first railway connection. Local enterprise had built the line but it was worked from the first by the South Western and taken over in 1874.

On the other side of Bournemouth there was dissatisfaction with the Poole branch, which actually ended at Hamworthy on the wrong side of the water. A new branch was therefore built from New Poole Junction (Broadstone) which followed the eastern side of Holes Bay and ran through Poole and Parkstone to a terminus in Bournemouth called Bournemouth West. It was opened on 15 June 1874.

Now that Bournemouth had two stations with no connection between them the question of joining them became a lively issue of local politics, with different views on the route to be taken through the town and the site of a new station to replace

Left:
**An Adams 'Radial' 4-4-2T built by Neilson in 1885, heads a Southampton-Weymouth stopping train near Moreton. Note the six-wheeled passenger brake with a raised lookout next to the engine.**
The Bucknall Collection/ Ian Allan Library

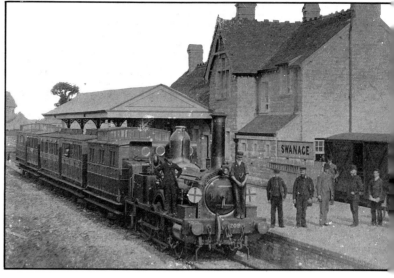

the old East terminus. A plan was finally agreed and the connecting line opened on 20 July 1885. Swanage had been served by rail since 30 May when the branch from Wareham was opened. The new through station in Bournemouth, more centrally situated than the former terminus, kept the name Bournemouth East until it was changed to Bournemouth Central on 1 May 1899.

The drawback of the detour via Ringwood to reach Christchurch remained — a legacy of the 'Corkscrew'. Work on a direct line from Brocken-hurst to Christchurch began in August 1884. Opening was delayed by a slip in the 60ft high embankment at Sway but all was ready for public services to begin on 6 March 1888. On the same day two short links in the Bournemouth rail network came into use which allowed through running from Waterloo to Weymouth via the new East station, avoiding Bournemouth West. The distance from Waterloo to Bournemouth was shortened by 8 miles.

Dorchester remained a terminus from the opening of 'Castleman's Corkscrew' in 1847 until the Great Western line from Westbury and Yeovil was opened to Weymouth in 1857. The South Western then exercised the running powers to Weymouth which it had been granted in the Act for the Southampton-Dorchester line. A connection ½ mile long branched southwards just on the London side of the terminus to join the Great Western at Dorchester Junction. There was a down platform on this connecting spur but all up trains had to clear the points at the north end of the spur and set back into the platform of the old terminus. This arrangement lasted into British Railways days.

The Great Western laid mixed gauge for the South Western trains, and the South Western accommodated the Great Western similarly with mixed gauge for 8 miles on its own line from Dorchester towards Wareham. This seems to have been to fulfil an agreement which settled earlier

Above:
**Reconstruction of Waterloo Station is well under way as this Bournemouth express departs, behind Drummond 'T14' 'Paddlebox' No 443 in 1909.**
L&GRP (4069)

Below right:

**A down Bournemouth express races through Earlsfield behind Urie mixed traffic 'H15' 4-6-0 No 482** Real Photographs (T6035)

disputes with the Great Western in the area rather than for any practical purpose. It will be recalled that Castleman had once approached the Great Western to work his line from Dorchester to Southampton and took a high-handed line with the South Western. He was later appeased with a seat on the South Western Board in 1855 and became Chairman of the company in 1862.

The Southampton-Dorchester line brought the South Western a new route to the Isle of Wight. An independent company opened a branch from Brockenhurst to Lymington in 1858 and a year later acquired the ferry operating between there and Yarmouth in the Island. The branch became South Western property in 1879 and in 1883 the company was asked to take over the ferries. A year later the branch was extended from Lymington Town to Lymington Pier. Yarmouth was without a railway until the opening of the Freshwater, Yarmouth & Newport line in 1890. Shortly before World War 1 there was a proposal for a tunnel under the Solent with a line connecting the South Western at Lymington with the Freshwater, Yarmouth & Newport at Yarmouth but it lapsed in the war years. After Grouping the scheme came up again. By that time the Southern Railway had made considerable investment in piers and ships to improve its services to the Island and expenditure on a Solent tunnel was ruled out.

# To Devon and Cornwall

While the London & South Western Railway still went no further west than Dorchester and Salisbury the company began to seek influence further afield. It became involved in various schemes in Devon and Cornwall to secure territory before the area was monopolised by broad gauge interests. As well as investing in harbour improvements at Stonehouse Pool, Plymouth, in 1846 the company purchased the Bodmin & Wadebridge Railway. This small standard gauge concern had opened its line in 1834, comprising what it regarded as its main line from Wadebridge to Wenford Bridge and a short branch to Bodmin. Wenford Bridge never saw regular passenger trains but served agricultural requirements and a small mining industry. In 1845 the broad gauge Cornwall Railway offered to buy the line as an extension of its proposed branch to Bodmin. Another offer came from the Cornwall & South Devon Railway which was planning a standard gauge line from Falmouth via Wadebridge to Exeter and had the backing of the South Western. The Bodmin & Wadebridge favoured the Cornwall & South Devon but this company failed to get its Bill through Parliament, whereupon the South Western stepped in and became the owner of a remote outpost which was not linked with the parent system for another 50 years. The first connection of the Bodmin & Wadebridge with the main railway network, in fact, was with the Great Western Railway in 1887 when a branch was opened from the GWR at Bodmin Road to a separate station in Bodmin, together with a connecting line from the GWR station to the Bodmin & Wadebridge at Boscarne Junction. This enabled the Great Western to operate a train service between Bodmin and Wadebridge interspersed with the B&W trains.

*Continued on page 35*

Above:
**An up West of England express leaves Salisbury in 1906 double-headed by two Adams locomotives. In front is 'T3' No 574 which is piloting 'X6' No 659. Double-heading was not a common sight in Drummond's time.** L&GRP (2709)

Right:
**Drummond 'G14' No 457, built at Nine Elms in 1908, speeds westward with a down express between Wilton and Dinton.**
The Bucknall Collection/Ian Allan Library

Top:
**Another double-headed train seen near Sherborne, headed by two Adams locomotives with '460' 4-4-0 No 472 leading and 'T3' 4-4-0 No 573 behind.** L&GRP (4684)

Above:
**Adams 'T3' No 568 nears the end of the long descent of the famous Honiton Bank and is seen passing through Seaton Junction at speed with an up West of England express. This view shows the original layout of the station; to the left of the signalbox is the branch line to Seaton.**
L&GRP (5580)

**JULY, 1867.**

**TIME TABLES**

OF THE

**LONDON**

AND

**SOUTH WESTERN**

**Railway and Steam Packets.**

THE DIRECT LINE TO EXETER, YEOVIL, BARNSTAPLE, BIDEFORD, AND THE WEST OF ENGLAND.

This Railway and its Branches communicate (see Map within) with the suburbs of London celebrated for their picturesque beauty, viz., Richmond, Windsor, Kew, and the Valley of the Thames, Virginia Water, Wokingham, Reading, Ewell, Epsom, Leatherhead, Hampton Court, Kingston, Claremont, &c.; also with Guildford, Midhurst, Portsmouth, Stokes Bay, Gosport, Winchester, Southampton, Salisbury, Direct Portsmouth Line, Third Class, Gillingham, Sherborne, Yeovil, Crewkerne, Axminster, Honiton, Exeter, Exmouth, North Devon, South Devon and the West of England, Lymington, the Isle of Wight, Blandford, Bournemouth, Dorchester, Weymouth, Glastonbury, Wells, Highbridge, Burnham for Cardiff, &c.

**FARES BETWEEN LONDON, JERSEY, GUERNSEY, PARIS, AND ST. MALO.**

| The Cheap & Picturesque Route FROM | SINGLE. Available for 4 Days. | | | RETURN. Available for One Month. | | |
|---|---|---|---|---|---|---|
| | 1st Cl. | 2nd Cl. | 3rd Cl. | 1st Cl. | 2nd Cl. | 3rd Cl. |
| London to Paris, or Paris to London | 28/0 | 20/0 | 16/0 | 50/0 | 36/0 | 28/0 |
| London to Guernsey Jersey, and St. Malo, or Guernsey, Jersey, and St. Malo to London | 31/0 | 21/0 | ... | 45/0 | 35/0 | ... |

For full particulars of Times of Trains and Service of Steam Boats, see pages 6, 7, 8, & 9.

| | Page |
|---|---|
| Saturday Cheap Tickets | 3 |
| Additional Third Class Trains and Third Class Return Tickets between Southampton and London | |
| Great Western Line Through Tickets | 3 |
| North Western Line Through Tickets | 3 |
| Isle of Wight, via Portsmouth | 4 |
| Thro' Fares between London & Ryde | 4 |
| Direct Portsmouth Line, Third Class Trains | 4 |
| Isle of Wight via Southampton | 4 |
| Through Fares between London & Cowes | 5 |
| Cowes and Newport Railway | 5 |
| Isle of Wight, via Lymington and Yarmouth | 5 |
| Southampton and Netley Line | 5 |
| Steam Packet Time Tables | 6 |
| Havre-de-Grace and Paris, &c. | 6 & 7 |
| Guernsey and Jersey | 6 & 7 |
| Trains to Aldershot Camp | 8 & 9 |
| Cheap Trains—Alton, Guildford, and Godalming Branches | 10 |
| Guernsey and Jersey | 11 |
| Thro' Tickets and Trains to and from South Devon Line | 29 |
| Exeter and Exmouth Trains | 30 |
| Wimbledon, Mitcham, Croydon, Surbiton and Hampton Court Trains | 30 |
| Trains | 31 |
| Wimbledon, Epsom, Leatherhead, Surbiton and Hampton Court Trains | 32 33 |
| Loop—Windsor, Kingston and Thames Valley Lines Trains (Week Days) | 34, 35 |
| Loop—Windsor, Kingston and Thames Valley Lines Trains (Sundays) | 36, 37 |
| Trains from Ludgate Hill to Hounslow, Kingston, &c. | 38 |
| Trains to Kingston, Hounslow, &c. | 39 |
| Trains to stations, Wokingham, and Reading Lines | 40 |
| New Communication between North Western, South Western, and South Eastern Lines, and between Waterloo and Cannon Streets | 41 |

| | Page |
|---|---|
| Trains between Basingstoke & Oxford, Leamington, Birmingham, &c., via Reading & Gt. Western Railway | 42 |
| Through Fares between Great Western and South Western Lines | 43 |
| Trains to and from London, Southampton, Dorchester and Weymouth | 43 |
| Trains between Southampton, Portsmouth, Brighton, Hastings, and Salisbury, Bristol, Bath &c. | 44 |
| Through Tickets between North Western Line and Channel Islands | 45 |
| Havre and South Western Lines, &c. | 46 |
| Thro' Trains between Southampton, Salisbury, &c., and Brighton, Hastings, &c. | 46 |
| Through Fares—South Coast & South Western, via Havant | 47 |
| Through Fares between Harra and Great Western Line | 47 |
| Trains between Sherborne and Yeovil | 48 |
| Cheap Market Tickets | 48 |
| Fares | 49 |
| Season Tickets | 50, 51 & 72 |
| Parcel Rates | 53 & 55 |
| Conveyance from Stations | 55 & 56 |
| Coach arrangements to and from South Tawton, Launceston, &c., worthy, &c. | 56 57 |
| Notice to Passengers | 57 |
| Charges for Exceptional Articles and Animals | 58, 59 |
| Bye Laws | 61 |
| Particulars of Goods Department | 68 |

PUBLISHED BY WATERLOW & SONS.] **PRICE ONE PENNY.** [CARPENTERS' HALL, LONDON WALL.

For Family, Tourist, and Excursion Tickets, see Yellow Pages.

Above:
**Until the opening of the new station at Bodmin in November 1895, the original terminus was at Bodmin Wharf. This view shows the scene in the late 1880s looking towards the end of the line.**
L&GRP (5447)

Below:
**A passenger train made from First, Second and Third Class rolling stock headed by the B&WR 0-4-0ST *Bodmin*, is seen at Bodmin Sand Drops, outside the old terminus. The gentlemen in the Third Class open wagon are the Directors of the LSWR seen paying a visit to the line in 1886.**
L&GRP (6011)

Above:
**One of the three well tanks shunts china clay wagons at Wenford Bridge in May 1959. The open wagons will be filled with loose clay, while the best quality clay will be loaded into the box van.**
Real Photographs Co (K3984)

The Bodmin & Wadebridge Railway Company (B&WR) was incorporated in 1832 and was opened to traffic in July 1834, four years before the L&SR. It was built to transport sea sand dredged from the Camel Estuary for conversion into fertiliser, and to bring ore mined at Wenford to Wadebridge. There were no great engineering works on the line, the route followed the eastern bank of the River Camel for the greater part of its distance. A gradient of 1 in 40 marked the approach to the terminus at Bodmin, almost 300ft above sea level. The B&WR was the first railway in the West of England to be authorised for locomotive haulage. Passenger traffic did not receive much consideration, as was the custom on these early lines. An imaginative plan was adopted for working passenger trains and goods trains between Bodmin and Wadebridge on alternate days of the week. At first trains stopped at any point along the line, an arrangement that saved the company the expense of having to erect and maintain stations, as well as being convenient for the public. Third Class passengers were conveyed in open vehicles, while Second and First Class passengers enjoyed the comparative luxury of a closed type of carriage. The revenue earned by the company never attained a very high figure and prospects of an increase were remote. The proprietors began to consider selling the whole concern to the promoters of the various ambitious railway schemes in Cornwall at that time. After many abortive offers the LSWR came to the rescue in 1846, and with commend-

## SOUTHERN RAILWAY

# CENTENARY
OF THE
## BODMIN
AND
## WADEBRIDGE
RAILWAY
1834-1934

*by courtesy of The Railway Magazine*

able foresight purchased a line that was, at the time, more than 200 miles away from its own rails. The line remained isolated for many years, and it was not until 1887 that the GWR, by constructing a short branch from their terminus at Bodmin to the B&WR at Boscarne, made it possible to work the railway on behalf of the company. This was a practice that was to continue until 1 June 1895 when the LSWR reached its remote offspring at Wadebridge, by means of the North Cornwall line from Launceston, The extension to Padstow was opened to traffic on 27 March 1899, making this the South Western's most westerly destination.

Top right:

**A frequent passenger service was operated up until October 1966. The Southern served all stations between Bodmin and Padstow, with connections at Wadebridge for Okehampton, Exeter and Waterloo. The GWR also ran a passenger service to Padstow, joining the line at Boscarne Junction and running non-stop between their station, Bodmin General, and Wadebridge. In this view 'O2' No 30200 leaves Dunmere Halt for Bodmin in 1950.** L&GRP (24509)

Right:

**The water tank at Pencarrow Woods was unique to the Wenford line, in that it was fed by gravity from a nearby stream. In this view No 30585 takes on water on its way to Wenford Bridge in 1950.**
Real Photographs (K3982)

3rd-SINGLE SINGLE 3rd
Launceston to Launceston
Launceston
Wadebridge Wadebridge
Wadebridge
**WADEBRIDGE**
W 4/11 Fare 4/11 W
For Conditions see over For Conditions see over

3854 3854

34

The South Western proposed to link up with its West Country allies through Exeter and had backed the Exeter & Crediton Railway. There was much controversy, however, over the route to be adopted to reach Exeter. 'Corkscrew' Castleman urged an extension from Dorchester in opposition to a broad gauge line via Dorchester from Westbury to Exeter. The broad gauge scheme was turned down on the condition that the South Western introduced a Bill for its Dorchester-Exeter line in the next session of Parliament. But these were troubled times. The country had barely emerged from the hysteria of the Railway Mania, dividends were falling and shareholders becoming wary of plans for further expenditure. When the proposed Bill was submitted for shareholders' approval at a special meeting on 15 November 1853 it was turned down. The company was lucky in that in a rapidly changing situation its commitment to build the Dorchester-Exeter line was quietly forgotten.

Two important developments helped to suppress further demands for extending to Exeter from Dorchester. Some of the Board had always favoured an extension westward from Salisbury, and a branch from Basingstoke that would provide a more direct route to the city from London than the existing one via Eastleigh was well advanced. A Salisbury & Yeovil Railway Company had been in existence since 1848 but had not previously exercised its powers. The approach of the South Western from Basingstoke encouraged it to begin construction on 3 April 1856. In the same year the South Western, having retreated thankfully from the Dorchester-Exeter scheme, applied for powers to build a line from Yeovil to Exeter. It was a

better proposition than the Dorchester route which would have involved 8 miles at 1 in 80 between Dorchester and Axminster, in the hills around Bridport, whereas from Yeovil to Exeter there would have to be only 3 miles at that gradient.

The Salisbury-Yeovil line was completed to its terminus at Yeovil Town in June 1860. The South Western's line to Exeter left the Salisbury & Yeovil at Bradford Abbas Junction. A little further west, at Yeovil Junction, there was a curve which joined the line to Yeovil Town at Yeovil Upper Junction. By means of this triangle of lines Yeovil Town could be approached from either direction, or trains could by-pass it by travelling direct between Bradford Abbas and Yeovil Junction. In later years the portion of the old Salisbury & Yeovil line between Bradford Abbas Junction and Yeovil Upper Junction was removed and the South Western served Yeovil by branch line trains from Yeovil Junction.

At Templecombe in 1862 the Dorset Central Railway (later Somerset & Dorset) passed under the Salisbury & Yeovil line. A curve connected the two lines, the junction with the Salisbury & Yeovil facing towards Salisbury. From 1863 to 1867 a shuttle service operated between the Upper station on the Salisbury & Yeovil and the Somerset &

Below:
**A massive 'F13' — No 333, built in 1905 — prepares to leave Exeter Queen Street with an up express when only a few months old. In the bay platform is a train for the Exmouth branch.**
L&GRP (25987)

Dorset station on the lower level, an operation involving two reversals. In 1870 this connection was replaced by a new line 67ch long called the Templecombe Junction Railway which left the Somerset & Dorset at a point north of that company's station and ran into the Upper station. The connection of the older curve with the main line was taken out and the remainder of the track was used as a siding. S&D trains booked to call at Templecombe ran into the Upper station and reversed out if coming from the north or pulled up past the junction points and backed in if coming from the south. It was an awkward operation. The writer has very distant memories of a journey from Honiton to Bournemouth West via Templecombe on a hot summer evening in stuffy non-corridor coaches, during which irascibility among the adults increased at every stop, and they seemed innumerable. Painful as it must be for those who revere the now-vanished line today, it must be admitted that at that time the initials S&D were popularly interpreted as standing for 'Slow and Dirty'.

The South Western's line from Yeovil to Exeter was opened throughout on 18 July 1860. Exeter enthusiastically welcomed the arrival of the standard gauge and the establishment of a shorter route from London than that offered by the Great Western and Bristol & Exeter companies. The distances were 171½ miles from Waterloo and 194 miles from Paddington.

West of Yeovil the Exeter line draws closer to the coast as it approaches the wide sweep of Lyme Bay. Over the years a number of branches were

Above:
**On the Exmouth branch c1910, a down train from Exeter passes along the south bank of the Exe Estuary between Woodbury Road and Lympstone, headed by an Adams 'O2' 0-4-4T.**
The Bucknall Collection/ Ian Allan Library

Right:
**Mixed gauge on the North Devon line survived until 1892; at Crediton standard gauge Beattie 2-4-0 No 48 *Hercules*, built at Nine Elms in 1851, heads a train for Barnstaple.** L&GRP (15962)

Above:
**An unidentified Adams 4-4-0 speeds an up express through Dartmoor across Fatherford viaduct, to the east of Okehampton.**
The Bucknall Collection/Ian Allan Library

opened to serve resorts along the Dorset and Devon coastline, beginning with the Exmouth branch. The dates of opening were:

| | |
|---|---|
| Exmouth Junction to Exmouth | 1 May 1863 |
| Colyton (later Seaton Junction) to Seaton | 16 March 1868 |
| Sidmouth Junction to Sidmouth | 6 July 1874 |
| Axminster-Lyme Regis | 23 August 1903 |

In 1897 a line to Budleigh Salterton was opened from Tipton St Johns on the Sidmouth branch. It was extended to Exmouth on 1 June 1903, shortening the journey from London compared with travelling via Exeter. Through coaches for Sidmouth and Exmouth were separated and combined at Tipton St Johns, where some interesting shunting operations could be observed on summer afternoons and a puzzled voice was once heard asking, 'What shall us do with this 'un George?' 'Put 'un on be'ind' was the reply, and another carriage was duly sent on its way to its labelled destination.

Only the branch from Exmouth Junction to Exmouth survives. The others live on in pleasant memories of summer holidays in the days before the annual break was as likely to be taken in Benidorm or the Seychelles as round our own coastline. All but forgotten except by the locals, one suspects, is the 3-mile branch from Chard Junction to Chard where it connected with a Great Western branch from Taunton via Ilminster. Yet it was an early addition to the system, having been opened on 8 May 1863.

Once established at Queen Street station, Exeter, the South Western was within hail of St Davids, where mixed gauge had been laid for Exeter & Crediton trains. The line to Crediton branched from the Bristol & Exeter at Cowley Bridge Junction, 1½ miles on the Taunton side of Exeter. A connection from Queen Street to St Davids was opened on 1 February 1862. The short distance between the stations and the difference in level made a gradient of 1 in 37 necessary, falling towards St Davids. On the same date the South Western took over the Exeter & Crediton. From Crediton the North Devon Railway continued to Barnstaple and Bideford, and by March 1863 mixed gauge had been laid to both places. South Western trains eventually reached the coast at Ilfracombe by an extension from Barnstaple opened on 20 July 1874.

The prime West Country target of the South Western at this time, however, was Plymouth. Truro was at one time a more distant goal, but was not realised. Access to Plymouth was to be by the Okehampton Railway which was given powers in 1865 to build a line from Coleford Junction, near Yeoford on the Exeter & Crediton, via Okehampton, to join the broad gauge Launceston & South Devon at Lydford. The Okehampton company was acquired by the South Western in 1871 and renamed the Devon & Cornwall Railway.

The Launceston & South Devon was a branch of the South Devon Railway which left the main line at Tavistock Junction and ran via Tavistock and Lydford to Launceston. Its Act required it to provide mixed gauge when requested to do so by

the Devon & Cornwall. The request came when the Devon & Cornwall's line from Okehampton reached Lydford in October 1874. Mixed gauge was laid and from 17 May 1876 South Western trains reached Plymouth via Tavistock. After joining the main line from Newton Abbot they travelled by running powers through North Road station to their own terminus at Devonport.

A single-track branch such as the Launceston line, shared with the trains of another company, was not the best basis for developing a competitive service. Some years later an alternative route from Lydford was provided by the Plymouth, Devonport & South Western Junction Railway. This line, opened on 1 June 1890, was worked from the first by the South Western. From Lydford to Tavistock it closely paralleled the South Devon (by now GWR) line but then diverged westward to Bere Alston, finally approaching Plymouth through Devonport where a new through station was built. South Western trains continued through Plymouth North Road to their own terminus at Friary, formerly a goods station. The South Western route to Plymouth therefore had two 'contraflow' sections — at Exeter and Plymouth. At both places their up and down trains ran in opposite directions to the corresponding services of the Great Western Railway.

Until the Great Western opened its Westbury route in 1905 the South Western had the advantage in distance from London. Waterloo to Plymouth was 229½ miles, and Paddington to Plymouth 246½ miles but the South Western route was more steeply graded. On the Okehampton line there were long stretches at 1 in 77 and a summit at 950ft. Between Yeovil Junction and Exeter, however, an excellent alignment enabled drivers to take advantage of steep down grades to rush a bank ahead. In the 1890 summer timetable the 11.00 from Waterloo made the journey to Plymouth in 5hr 45min, saving 30min compared with the previous timing and beating the Great Western's 'Flying Dutchman' by 25min. But the Great Western already had an answer for on 2 June 1890 it put on a new train from Paddington which, by omitting stops at Bath, Taunton and west of Exeter, reached Plymouth in 5hr 35min.

Competition for Plymouth traffic intensified when transatlantic liners began putting passengers ashore by tender at Plymouth, enabling them to reach London sooner by rail than if they stayed on board until Southampton. The South Western had already invested in improvements at Stonehouse Pool, and to provide for the new traffic now built a short branch to the quayside. From 1904 Ocean Specials for liner passengers were run to Waterloo.

Far left:
**Still in LSWR livery, a Drummond 'C8' class engine, built at Nine Elms in 1898, crosses the impressive Meldon viaduct to the west of Okehampton in June 1924.**
The Bucknall Collection/ Ian Allan Library

Left:
**Adams 'X6' 4-4-0 No 660 joins the GWR main line at Lipson Junction for its run into Plymouth North Road with an up express.**
The Bucknall Collection/ Ian Allan Library

Below left:
**The Plymouth Devonport & South Western Railway (PD&SWR) opened in 1890 and was leased to the LSWR from the start, enabling them to enter Plymouth using their own main line via Tavistock, Bere Alston and St Budeaux. In March 1908 the PD&SWR opened and worked a branch line from Bere Alston to Callington. In this view a PD&SWR 0-6-0 _A. S. Harris_ shunts a mineral train at Gunnislake.** Lens of Sutton

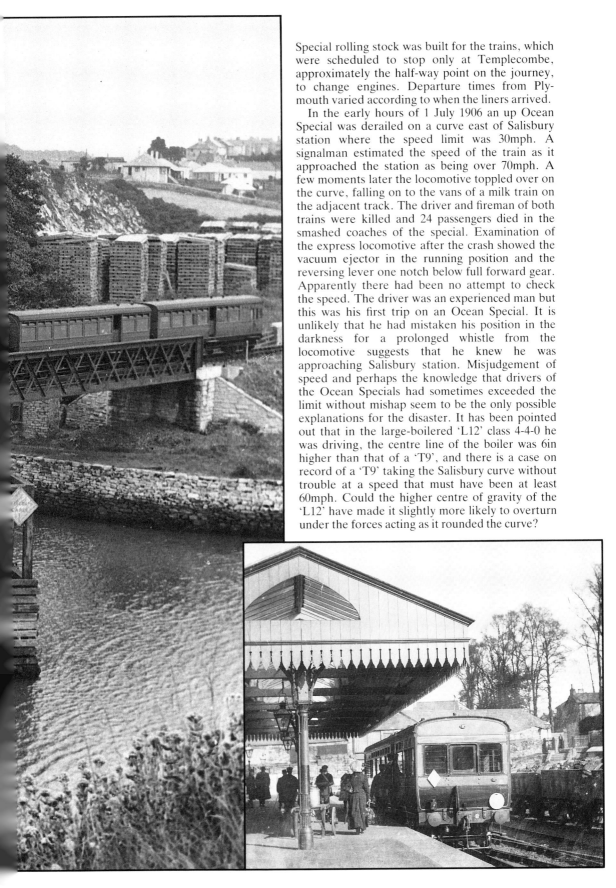

Special rolling stock was built for the trains, which were scheduled to stop only at Templecombe, approximately the half-way point on the journey, to change engines. Departure times from Plymouth varied according to when the liners arrived.

In the early hours of 1 July 1906 an up Ocean Special was derailed on a curve east of Salisbury station where the speed limit was 30mph. A signalman estimated the speed of the train as it approached the station as being over 70mph. A few moments later the locomotive toppled over on the curve, falling on to the vans of a milk train on the adjacent track. The driver and fireman of both trains were killed and 24 passengers died in the smashed coaches of the special. Examination of the express locomotive after the crash showed the vacuum ejector in the running position and the reversing lever one notch below full forward gear. Apparently there had been no attempt to check the speed. The driver was an experienced man but this was his first trip on an Ocean Special. It is unlikely that he had mistaken his position in the darkness for a prolonged whistle from the locomotive suggests that he knew he was approaching Salisbury station. Misjudgement of speed and perhaps the knowledge that drivers of the Ocean Specials had sometimes exceeded the limit without mishap seem to be the only possible explanations for the disaster. It has been pointed out that in the large-boilered 'L12' class 4-4-0 he was driving, the centre line of the boiler was 6in higher than that of a 'T9', and there is a case on record of a 'T9' taking the Salisbury curve without trouble at a speed that must have been at least 60mph. Could the higher centre of gravity of the 'L12' have made it slightly more likely to overturn under the forces acting as it rounded the curve?

After the accident the Ocean Special schedules were extended and stops at Exeter and Salisbury were imposed. Four sleeping cars were built for the greater comfort of passengers travelling overnight. They only worked on the South Western for a short time for in 1910, when all competitive traffic was pooled by the GWR and the LSWR, the Ocean Specials were taken off.

Plymouth and Exeter were in shared territory but the north coast of Cornwall was a South Western preserve. Powers to build a line to the Cornish coast at Bude had been given to the Okehampton Railway in 1865 but these 41 miles were not opened throughout until 10 August 1898. The branch left the main line to Lydford and Plymouth at Meldon Junction, some 2½ miles west of Okehampton. At Halwill Junction a branch diverged to serve Padstow. It was opened to Launceston on 21 July 1886 and extended to Padstow in stages. Between Camelford and Delabole the railway was not far inland from Tintagel Head where tradition placed the castle in which King Arthur was born. In later years the Southern Railway found a treasury of resonant and romantic names for its 'King Arthur' class locomotives in the stories of the king and his court. On 1 June 1895 the line joined the Bodmin &

Wadebridge Railway a little to the east of Wadebridge station. Construction continued westward, Wadebridge became a through station instead of a terminus, and on 27 March 1899 the railway reached Padstow.

When the line to Bude was built the Okehampton Railway was given powers for a branch northwards from Halwill Junction to Torrington. They were not exercised, and the first railway in Torrington was a southward extension from Bideford opened on 1 July 1872. With an outlet only via Bideford and Barnstaple, some traffic from Torrington had to make a long detour to reach its destination. The question of closing the gap to Halwill Junction, only 20 miles to the south arose again and in 1914 a North Cornwall & Devon Railway Company was formed to build a line. Clay and lignite workings were to be the principal source of traffic but passengers would benefit as well from shorter journeys. Indeed, the promoters looked forward to Halwill Junction 'becoming one of the largest and most important junctions on a single line in the United Kingdom'. Construction was delayed by the war and did not begin until 30 June 1922. By the time it was completed on 27 July 1925 the South Western had merged into the Southern Railway and the line was leased to the new Group.

Right:
**Three of the famous Beattie 2-4-0WTs served out most of their lives in Cornwall on the Bodmin & Wadebridge line, having been found to be the only suitable engines for the mineral line to Wenford Bridge. Between their normal duties they often undertook local passenger work, as in this view of No 0298 seen near Padstow in 1921.**
H. C. Casserley

Below right:
**Padstow, 259 miles from Waterloo, was the LSWR's most distant destination for through workings. Here an Adams '460' class 4-4-0 leaves with an up 'Cornwall Express'.** L&GRP (8092)

# Links with other Lines

From the early days of the railway the management was interested in connections between its system and lines to the Midlands and North. When the London & Birmingham Railway proposed a branch from Rugby to Oxford and Didcot, the South Western planned a branch to Didcot from Basingstoke in the interests of providing 'a direct north and south communication by the narrow gauge all the way from Aberdeen to the south'. Neither scheme was sanctioned, however, but the Great Western was authorised to build a line from Reading to Basingstoke. This decision rankled with the South Western. The permission was granted, said Sam Fay in *A Royal Road*, 'in accord with the absurd ideas of the Board of Trade', and he castigated the Board's 'idiotic awards, which had caused useless expense and inconvenience to the public at large'. In later years there was much argument between the South Western and the Great Western over the Didcot, Newbury & Southampton Railway which was opened to its own station in Winchester on 1 May 1885 and extended to join the South Western at Shawford Junction on 1 October 1891 with running powers to Southampton Docks. The distance from Didcot to Southampton by this route was six miles shorter than via Reading and Basingstoke.

From 1 August 1891 the Midland & South Western Junction Railway exercised running powers over the South Western from Red Posts Junction, near Andover Junction on the Salisbury line, to Southampton Docks via Andover Town, Romsey and Redbridge. At its northern end the line joined the Great Western at Andoversford, near Cheltenham, and running powers to Cheltenham (Midland) enabled through services to be worked between Southampton and the North via Derby.

The connection with the Somerset & Dorset Joint Railway (S&D) at Broadstone Junction, opened on 14 December 1885, created the South Western's most important link with the Midlands and the North. The Somerset & Dorset had reached Bath and a junction with the Midland Railway on 20 July 1874. A year later the Midland and the South Western leased the line jointly. At that time the southern end of the S&D joined the South Western at Wimborne, where reversal was necessary to reach Bournemouth. The curve to Broadstone Junction allowed trains to run direct. Among the through services by this route was a Manchester and Liverpool to Bournemouth train inaugurated in 1910 which after Grouping was named the 'Pines Express'.

The South Western had close ties with the Great Central Railway in Sam Fay, who had been Superintendent of the line before being appointed General Manager of the Great Central in 1902, and had served the South Western in other capacities earlier in his career. Soon after he took up his appointment with the Great Central a through service was inaugurated between Newcastle and Bournemouth. The train, which began running on 1 July 1902, followed the Great Central main line from Sheffield to Culworth Junction, south of Woodford & Hinton (later Woodford Halse), then took the branch to Banbury to join the Great Western. The route was then via Oxford, Didcot and Reading to join the South Western at Basingstoke. Fay's disgust at a line from Reading to Basingstoke being sanctioned rather than one from Didcot has been recorded earlier.

Two important links with other lines, of particular importance for freight movements, were established in the London area. On 15 February 1853 the North & South Western Junction Railway was opened between Kew and Willesden. Junctions at Kew connected with the South Western's Windsor Lines. From 1 October 1866 this network provided a 'back door' approach to London, avoiding the busy main line between Weybridge and Clapham. The North & South Western Junction (N&SWJ) line was primarily intended for the exchange of freight but the South Western was required to provide a passenger service for a short time. On 1 October 1868 the Midland Railway opened a branch from Brent Sidings, Cricklewood, to the N&SWJ at Old Oak Junction. Reciprocal arrangements allowed Midland trains to join the South Western, and South Western trains to run to Cricklewood.

The South Western had a one-sixth share in the West London Extension Railway which from 2 March 1863 provided a link between Clapham Junction and the Great Western and London & North Western Railways. The westward-facing connection with the South Western at Clapham was with the Windsor Lines. A branch from Kensington (Addison Road) on the West London line to Richmond via Turnham Green, Gunnersbury and Kew Gardens was opened on 1 January 1869.

## Suburban Routes

A characteristic of the South Western's suburban system in the London area was the network north of the main line, known collectively as the Windsor Lines. The name was first given to the separate tracks from Clapham Junction to Waterloo for trains of the Richmond service. The extension from Richmond to Datchet was opened on 22 August 1848 and onward to Windsor on 1 December 1849. The loop from Barnes to Hounslow via Brentford dates from 1 February 1850. From Waterloo to Staines the Windsor line became part of a route to Reading when a line from Staines to Wokingham was opened on 9 July 1856. Virginia Water on the Wokingham line was connected with the main line at Weybridge on 1 October 1866, providing the 'bypass' to London mentioned in the preceding section of this chapter. In later years a freight concentration yard was built at Feltham on the 'bypass' and completed in 1922 on the eve of Grouping.

To many travellers at Waterloo the Windsor Lines may well seem a railway apart, swinging away at Clapham Junction to platforms separated from the rest by sidings and reached by a long footbridge or subway. Staines to Windsor on the map today looks like a branch from a main line to Wokingham and Reading.

Kingston-on-Thames was first served by a station of its own on 1 July 1863 when a branch was

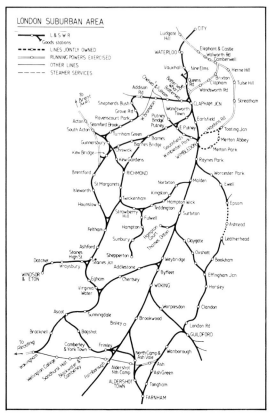

Below:
**The Addison Road-Richmond service, seen at Addison Road in 1872 was operated by this 2-4-0WT No 190, built by Beyer Peacock in 1864.**
LPC/Ian Allan Library

opened from Twickenham. The branch was extended to the main line at Malden (now New Malden) on 1 January 1869, enabling a 'round-about' service to be run from Waterloo in either direction via Twickenham, Kingston and Wimbledon. A branch from Shepperton to a triangular junction with the Twickenham-Kingston section at Strawberry Hill was opened on 1 November 1864. Shepperton trains could be routed via the Windsor Lines or via Wimbledon and Kingston. It was once

planned to extend the Shepperton line to Chertsey on the Virginia Water-Weybridge line but it did not materialise.

Two South Western suburban stations were served by trains of the Metropolitan District Railway. The District line joined the LSWR Kensington-Richmond branch at Studland Road Junction, Hammersmith, and from 1 June 1877 trains ran through from Mansion House to Richmond. Metropolitan District trains worked to Wimbledon from 3 June 1889, joining the South Western at East Putney. Powers to build the Wimbledon-East Putney line had been granted to the South Western subject to District trains having running powers. The branch was connected to the Windsor Lines at Point Pleasant Junction, between Clapham Junction and Barnes, by curves opened

Top:

**Many of the Adams 'T1' class engines were fitted for push-pull working and were used on many branch lines. Here No 367, built in 1896 at Nine Elms and still in LSWR livery, propels a train from the Chertsey branch at Virginia Water in 1926.**
H. C. Casserley

on 1 July 1889. Other branches from the main line were opened as follows:

| | |
|---|---|
| Surbiton-Hampton Court | 1 February 1849 |
| Raynes Park-Epsom | 4 April 1859 |
| Hampton Court Junction-Guildford via Cobham | 2 February 1885 |

The Epsom branch was extended to Leatherhead by a line worked jointly with the LBSCR although it was under South Western ownership from 1860. Both companies had separate stations at Epsom and Leatherhead. An extension was built from Leatherhead LSWR station to join the Guildford via Cobham line at Effingham Junction and brought into use on the same day that the line was opened. Guildford thereby gained three routes from Waterloo: via Woking and the Portsmouth Direct line; via Cobham; and via Epsom and Leatherhead. This was typical of the variety of the South Western suburban system.

Secondary lines west of Woking and Guildford hardly come into the suburban category but the opening of the branch from the main line at Pirbright Junction, Brookwood, to Aldershot and Farnham on 2 May 1870 must be included for its importance in providing a direct route from Waterloo to Aldershot, previously reached via Guildford. Joining the existing line to Alton at Farnham Junction, the new branch also connected with the alternative routes to Winchester via Alresford, and to Fareham via the Meon Valley line.

Bottom:
**An Adams '135' class No 144, built by Beyer Peacock in 1880, draws into Surbiton. Until 1863 this station was known as Kingston, or 'Kingston-upon-Railway' by the locals. In the background is the Southampton Railway Hotel.**
LPC/Ian Allan Library (1964)

# Electrification

For some years after its London Brighton & South Coast neighbour had begun electrifying in the London area the South Western continued working its suburban services with steam. The spreading network of electric tramways was eroding the traffic, but it was not until 1913 that the decision to electrify was taken. Alternating current systems at high voltage were in an early stage of development. In this country the only example outside London was on the Lancaster-Morecambe-Heysham lines of the Midland Railway but direct current at a nominal 600V had proved itself on underground railways in London and on suburban services based on Liverpool and Newcastle. The LBSC had chosen high-voltage ac with electrification of its main line to the coast in mind, balancing a lower cost for substations at 11,000V against the cost of overhead equipment. The South Western was not looking so far afield. In going for 600V dc the South Western took a step which in later years would set a pattern for all the railways south of London and in the end result in the anomaly of a system intended for the suburbs being extended over all the main lines to the southern coast, eventually reaching Weymouth, nearly 143 miles from Waterloo.

The first electric service was from Waterloo to Wimbledon via Point Pleasant Junction and East Putney, opened on 25 October 1915. The East Putney-Wimbledon section had already been electrified at 660V dc for the District trains. Between Wimbledon and East Putney positive and negative conductor rails were laid to meet the District Railway requirement of an insulated path for return current. Elsewhere only a positive conductor rail was provided, return current flowing through the motorcoach axles and wheels to the running rails. In those days electric railways had to generate their own power supplies. A power station was built at Durnsford Road, Wimbledon, from which three-phase current at 11,000V was distributed to the substations feeding the live rails. At the substations rotary machines converted the high-voltage ac into dc for the trains.

On 30 January 1916 electrification was extended to Kingston and over the Shepperton branch. The two routes to Kingston — via Richmond and via Wimbledon — were electrified so that a 'roundabout' service could be run, out one way and back the other. The Hounslow loop followed on 12 March, and the Hampton Court branch on 18 June. Among the preliminary works for the electrification was the construction of a flyover at Hampton Court Junction to take the trains to Hampton Court over the main lines. By this time the war was approaching a critical stage. It had

Above:
**An early view of the unit No E73, showing clearly its red oil tail lamp affixed above the buffer beam.** GEC Traction

Above:
**Two three-car sets are seen departing from Hounslow station on the Waterloo-Richmond-Hounslow service in the mid-1920s.**
Ian Allan Library

been planned to electrify the Guildford via Cobham line but after the live rail had reached Claygate on 20 November the work was suspended.

Rolling stock for the electric services was converted from non-corridor steam stock. The basic unit consisted of two motorcoaches and an intermediate trailer. Two units operated in multiple in busy periods. At a later stage the maximum train length was increased to eight coaches by coupling two additional trailers between a pair of units. With four 275hp motors per unit there was ample power for the longer trains and performance was lively. An editorial in *The Railway Gazette* looked forward to better schedules compared with the 'leisurely jog trot of the existing steam trains' and predicted that the South Western company's suburban traffic would be revolutionised. Control equipment was carried inside the motorcoaches in a compartment behind the cab. The contactors clicked loudly during acceleration, earning the trains the name 'nutcrackers'.

Accommodation was First and Third Class, omitting the seconds that were then provided in other South Western coaches. In some coaches a First Class smoking saloon occupied the space of three former compartments. It appeared, perhaps a little larger than life, on pictorial posters advertising the new services, giving an impression of similarity with the Blackpool 'Club' trains for Manchester businessmen, although without the refinement of a steward serving refreshments. Seating on both sides of the saloon faced inwards and there were seats across the ends so that the assembled City gentlemen were conveniently placed for discussing the price of Gilts or boardroom changes.

But the most characteristic feature of the new services was the regular-interval timetable. Travellers no longer had to look up a train but knew there would be one at their local station at set times throughout the day and that there would be convenient connections if a change was necessary on their journey. It was a doctrine of Herbert Walker, who became General Manager of the London & South Western Railway in 1912, that people did not like timetables and he stamped the same pattern on the Southern Electric of the postwar years of which he was the driving force.

It may seem surprising that the railway should launch a major electrification programme while Europe was in the grip of war, but it was in line with the 'business as usual' policy that was officially encouraged in the early years. The railway had already made a significant contribution to the war effort. Between 9 and 31 August 1914 it handled 711 special trains arriving at Southampton with men, horses and materials for the Expeditionary Force being despatched to France. On 23 August alone, 73 specials arrived at an average frequency of one every 15min. A Railway Executive Committee, formed in 1912, took over control of the railways on the outbreak of war. Herbert Walker succeeded to the chairmanship of this body in February 1914 and his work in the first critical phase was recognised by the award of a knighthood in the New Year Honours of 1915.

The rebuilding of Waterloo had begun before the outbreak of war. Involving a complete renewal of a once-sprawling and inconvenient station, it extended over 15 years. Completion was marked by a formal opening ceremony by Queen Mary on 21 March 1922. In the same year the great freight concentration and hump yard at Feltham was brought into use. Convenient connections with other railways north of the Thames gave further effect to a through communication policy which had been pursued from the early days. It was now the eve of Grouping. Soon the publicity organisation of the new Southern Railway, formed on 1 January 1923, would be urging the press to stop referring to the Southern constituents by their former company names. But with these two impressive reminders of a spirit of enterprise that flourished to the end, the traditions of the London & South Western Railway were secure.

---

Pamphlet No. 295.

# LONDON AND SOUTH WESTERN RAILWAY.

## INTRODUCTION OF

# ADDITIONAL ELECTRIC TRAINS

BETWEEN

## WATERLOO, WIMBLEDON, KINGSTON, SHEPPERTON, TWICKENHAM & RICHMOND,

AND ALTERATIONS CONSEQUENT THEREON,

## On SUNDAYS, commencing 4th June, 1916,

ALSO

# ALTERATIONS IN THE TRAIN SERVICE

## On WEEK=DAYS, commencing 5th June, 1916.

FOR FULL PARTICULARS, SEE FOLLOWING PAGES.

Above:
**Kitchener's famous Great War poster that appeared on many railway stations.**

Below:
**The response — men arrive for their training at Bisley during World War 1.** Lens of Sutton

The LSWR played a major role in troop and support movements during Britain's overseas campaigns and both world wars. In 1885 Queen Victoria opened two military camps, called North Camp and South Camp, built on heathland surrounding Aldershot. The railheads were at Farnborough on the main line and Tongham on the Alton line, and thus provided easy rail access to the Channel ports. The LSWR also built three short branch lines serving other military camps in the area. One, running from Brookwood to Bisley, Pirbright, Deepcut and Blackdown camps, was originally built to serve the National Rifle Association at Bisley. Opened in 1914, it was placed under the jurisdiction of the War Office for the training of regular troops, and became an important centre for small arms training. The 3-mile extension to Pirbright, Deepcut and Blackdown was built by German prisoners of war and was completed in 1917. The year 1902 saw the opening of the Amesbury and Military Camp Railway which left the West of England main line between Grateley and Porton. It was extended to Bulford in 1906. The third line — a 4.5-mile branch from Bentley, on the Alton line, to Bordon — opened in 1905 and eventually formed the northern link for the Longmoor Military Railway. During one 48hr period in September 1910 the LSWR moved 25,080 troops, 6,722 horses and 1,174 guns, and all done with the greatest efficiency.

In August 1911 the Under Secretary of State for War, Sir John Seely, called a meeting of the six major railway companies, which included the LSWR, to consider transport problems in times of war. For any preparations for war it was soon realised that the LSWR would occupy the key position and by late 1912 the Railway Executive Committee (REC) was set up. During the crisis of August 1914 the War Office gave the REC just 60hr to assemble enough locomotives and rolling stock to get the expeditionary forces to Southampton. By 9 August, 24hr ahead of schedule, the embarkation of troops had begun. By 31 August 711 special trains had arrived at Southampton Docks carrying 5,006 officers, 125,171 men, 38,805 horses, 344 guns, 1,574 other limbered vehicles, 277 motorcycles and 6,406 tons of stores. From the outbreak of World War 1, recognition of Southampton's strategical position and its ability to deal efficiently with all classes of traffic led to its designation as No 1 Military Port under Government control. The railways' busiest period of all was on 21 August when 73 special trains arrived at Southampton, with an average of one train arriving every 15min. Besides being a port for departures it was also the reception point for troops and supplies arriving from America and the Colonies. By the end of the war the following traffic had been handled:

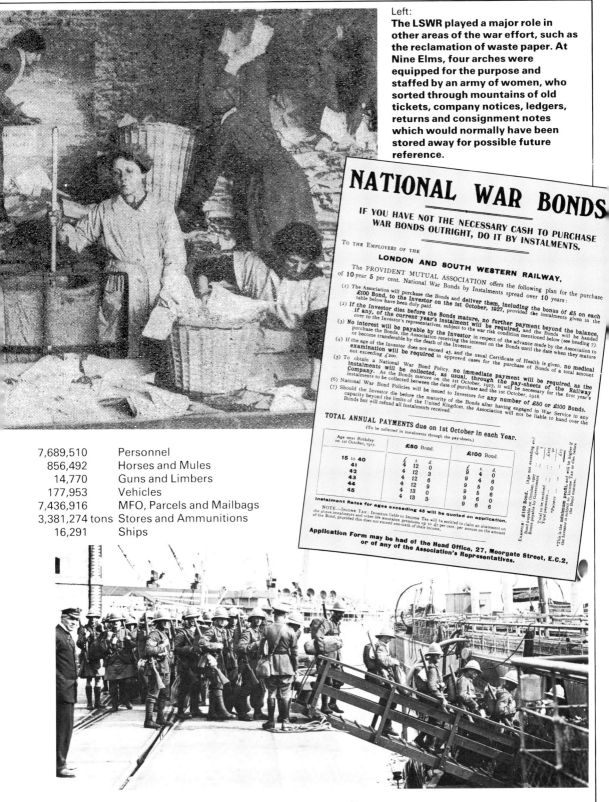

**Left:**
**The LSWR played a major role in other areas of the war effort, such as the reclamation of waste paper. At Nine Elms, four arches were equipped for the purpose and staffed by an army of women, who sorted through mountains of old tickets, company notices, ledgers, returns and consignment notes which would normally have been stored away for possible future reference.**

# NATIONAL WAR BONDS

### IF YOU HAVE NOT THE NECESSARY CASH TO PURCHASE WAR BONDS OUTRIGHT, DO IT BY INSTALMENTS.

To THE EMPLOYEES OF THE

## LONDON AND SOUTH WESTERN RAILWAY.

The PROVIDENT MUTUAL ASSOCIATION offers the following plan for the purchase of 10-year 5 per cent. National War Bonds by Instalments spread over 10 years:

(1) The Association will purchase the Bonds and deliver them, including the bonus of £5 on each £100 Bond, to the Investor on the 1st October, 1927, provided the instalments given in the table below have been duly paid.

(2) If the Investor dies before the Bonds mature, no further payment beyond the balance, if any, of the current year's instalment will be required, and the Bonds will be handed over to the Investor's representatives, subject to the war risk condition mentioned below.

(3) No interest will be payable by the Investor in respect of the advance made by the Association to purchase the Bonds, the Association receiving the interest on the Bonds until the date when they mature or become transferable by the death of the Investor.

(4) If the age of the Investor does not exceed 45, and the usual Certificate of Health is given, no medical examination will be required in approved cases for the purchase of Bonds of a total amount not exceeding £200.

(5) To obtain a National War Bond Policy, no immediate payment will be required, as the instalments will be collected, as usual, through the pay-sheets of the Railway Company. As the Bonds mature on the 1st October, 1927, it will be necessary for the first year's instalments to be collected between the date of purchase and the 1st October, 1918.

(6) National War Bond Policies will be issued to Investors for any number of £50 or £100 Bonds.

(7) Should the Investor die before the maturity of the Bonds after having engaged in War Service in any capacity beyond the limits of the United Kingdom, the Association will not be liable to hand over the Bonds but will refund all instalments received.

### TOTAL ANNUAL PAYMENTS due on 1st October in each Year.

(To be collected in instalments through the pay-sheets.)

| Age next Birthday on 1st October, 1917. | £50 Bond. | | | £100 Bond. | | |
|---|---|---|---|---|---|---|
| | £ | s. | d. | £ | s. | d. |
| 15 to 40 | 4 | 12 | 4 | 9 | 4 | 8 |
| 41 | 4 | 12 | 5 | 9 | 4 | 10 |
| 42 | 4 | 12 | 6 | 9 | 5 | 0 |
| 43 | 4 | 12 | 8 | 9 | 5 | 4 |
| 44 | 4 | 13 | 0 | 9 | 6 | 0 |
| 45 | 4 | 13 | 3 | 9 | 6 | 6 |

Instalment Rates for ages exceeding 45 will be quoted on application.

NOTE.—INCOME TAX: Investors liable to Income Tax will be entitled to claim an abatement on the above instalments and other life assurance premiums up to 4/7 per cent, per annum on the amount of the Bond, provided this does not exceed one-sixth of their income.

Application Form may be had of the Head Office, 27, Moorgate Street, E.C.2, or of any of the Association's Representatives.

| 7,689,510 | Personnel |
|---|---|
| 856,492 | Horses and Mules |
| 14,770 | Guns and Limbers |
| 177,953 | Vehicles |
| 7,436,916 | MFO, Parcels and Mailbags |
| 3,381,274 tons | Stores and Ammunitions |
| 16,291 | Ships |

**Above:**
**Troops embarking for the Middle East during World War 1, at Southampton's Outer Dock.**
Imperial War Museum

# Shipping Services

The fame of Southampton as a port for worldwide travel tended to overshadow the South Western's own marine activities. Since at first railways were not allowed to operate their own ships, a separate South Western Navigation Company was formed in 1845 to sail from Southampton to the Channel Islands, Le Havre and St Malo. Previously, mails for the Channel Islands had been carried by Post Office packets from Weymouth, but the contract was now given to the new company, which took over two wooden paddle steamers previously working from Weymouth and had a new iron ship, the *Wonder*, built for the Le Havre route. The Western Railway of France opened its line to Le Havre in 1847, enabling the South Western to provide a London-Paris overnight service. There is a scene in Zola's novel *La Bête Humaine*, where the early morning train from Le Havre to Paris is marooned in a snowdrift. Among the passengers are 'a large woman with two pretty fair-haired young girls, no doubt her daughters and all three

Below:
**The steamship *Hilda* at Guernsey Pier; in November 1905 she was lost off St Malo in a snowstorm.**

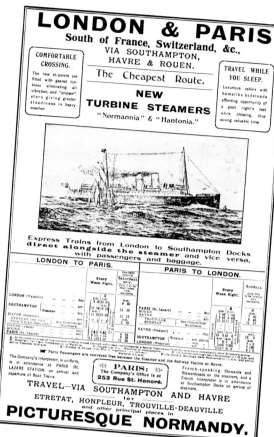

Left:
**The steamship *Princess Ena* at St Malo, the port for Brittany. Note the LSWR offices on the quayside.**
The *Railway Magazine*

certainly English'. One can imagine them coming from Waterloo, as well as the angry businessman returning from a visit to London who threatens to sue the company for failing to get him to Paris in time for a meeting. The St Malo service had more of a holiday atmosphere, and the connecting trains from Waterloo carried 'St Malo' destination boards as if no water lay between. Cherbourg and Granville were also served. The South Western Navigation Company, which was really only a convenient fiction to comply with the law, was absorbed by the railway company in 1862.

When the Great Western Railway reached Weymouth in 1857, and the South Western exercised its running powers from Dorchester, a service to the Channel Islands was started from the

Below:
**Sailings for Le Havre in 1860 were on Mondays, Wednesdays and Fridays departing from the Royal Pier by the *Alliance* or *Havre*; the fare was 21s First Class and 15s Second Class. In this view the PS *Alliance* is seen leaving the port of Le Havre.**
The Bucknall Collection/Ian Allan Library

P.S. "ALLIANCE". 1855.

LONDON & SOUTH WESTERN RAILWAY.

# LONDON
## AND
## PARIS
### & THE RIVIERA.

VIA SOUTHAMPTON AND HAVRE

CONNECTION between BOAT & TRAIN GUARANTEED.

CHEAPEST AND MOST COMFORTABLE NIGHT ROUTE IN LUXURIOUS MAIL STEAMERS.

WATERLOO STATION · CHAS. J. OWENS, General Manager.

sunk, three of them torpedoed and one being wrecked on the French coast when the light at La Hogue was extinguished as a war measure.

On the Isle of Wight services the ships on the Lymington-Yarmouth crossing belonged to the LSWR fleet but those between Portsmouth and Ryde were jointly owned by the South Western and the London Brighton & South Coast Railway.

Below:
**The paddle steamer *Duchess of Fife*, built in 1899, was one of five joint LSWR/LBSCR steamers, taken over by the SR in 1923, which operated the Isle of Wight services, sailing from Portsmouth Harbour-Ryde.** Real Photographs (S4062)

port by a Weymouth & Islands Steam Packet Company. The South Western countered the competition with its Southampton service by sending a ship from Southampton to work from Weymouth but it was returned to Southampton in 1860. In 1880 the Great Western bought the steamship company and so was in direct competition with the South Western for the Channel Islands traffic. The mails, however, remained with the South Western. From December 1899 the traffic was pooled between the two railways.

South Western ships sailed in some hazardous waters and there were disasters. On 30 September 1859 the steamer *Express* struck a rock near the Corbière lighthouse, Jersey, and was wrecked. The *Stella* struck the Black Rock, near the Casquets, on 30 March 1899 in heavy weather. The captain and 104 others were drowned. The most serious episode, claiming 128 lives, was when the *Hilda* struck a rock at the entrance to St Malo harbour during a snowstorm on 18 November 1905. There were further losses during World War 1 when four ships of the LSWR fleet were

Above:
**The SS *Cherbourg*, built in 1873, had a top speed of 12kt and is seen here at the port after which she was named. She was in service for 57 years before being broken up in 1930.**
The Bucknall Collection/Ian Allan Library

Below:
**In 1930-31 the Southern provided three new ships for the Channel Islands service. The *Isle of Jersey*, *Isle of Sark* and the *Isle of Guernsey* all had accommodation for 800 First Class and 600 Second Class passengers, in this view the *Isle of Guernsey* is seen passing Elizabeth Castle, Jersey.**

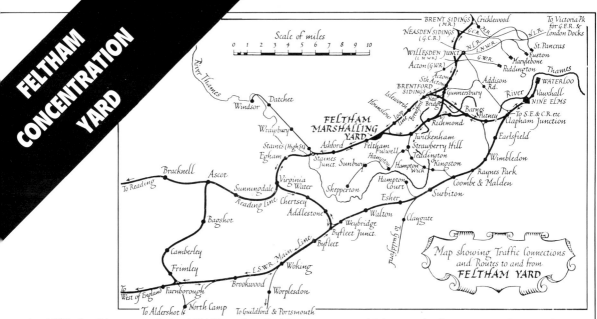

Map showing Traffic Connections and Routes to and from FELTHAM YARD

In 1918 the Directors of the LSWR took a bold step; by taking the advice of their General Manager Sir Herbert Walker, they authorised the construction of a totally new freight concentration yard on land north of Feltham station. It was to handle freight traffic between various parts of the LSWR system and the goods depot at Nine Elms, and would also deal with the heavy freight exchange traffic from other railway companies north of the Thames. Until then most marshalling yards had grown from small beginnings with additions being made here and there as traffic grew. The provision of a complete, well-planned yard gave the LSWR a common point from where all freight movement could be centred, with the exception of train-loads of perishable and other urgent traffic.

By 1922 the yard had been completed, at a cost of £250,000, having a total of 30 miles of single track. The above map shows how direct access could be made from any point on the system, and also routes to and from other companies north of the Thames. The yard was situated on the south side of the line. Up trains entered by facing points, entering on one of eight reception sidings, each of which could accommodate up to 68 wagons; this led to 16 roads of marshalling sidings. On the down side accommodation was slightly smaller, with six reception sidings leading to 17 marshalling sidings. The down yard had only to deal with local services from Nine Elms, branches in the London area and from the northern lines. A second group of sidings was provided at the down end of the yard for sorting wagons into station order. On arrival, main line engines were sent to the shed or turned around for their return. An engine was attached to the rear of the train which then pushed the wagons over one of the two humps, where they could be marshalled by gravity. The operation of

**A view of the western end of the yard, seen here in 1922; the new steel girder bridge was erected to enable track widening.** The *Railway Magazine*

points was done electrically from a 35-lever all-electric signalbox, situated near each hump. Movement into and out of the yard was controlled by Feltham Junction signalbox at the London end, or by Feltham station East signalbox at the other end.

The yard was also provided with an engine shed which had accommodation for 42 tender locomotives and a coaling stage with a capacity of 12,000 tons of coal. A wagon repair shop, cattle pens, and transfer goods shed were also provided, while other buildings included mess rooms and a hostel with sleeping accommodation. From the Lookout Tower the yard master could keep in contact by phone with all parts of the yard, and also principal stations on the LSWR. The whole yard was electrically lit for night working.

Right:
**An interior view of Feltham East signalbox, which controlled movements at the country end of the yard.** Ian Allan Library

Below:
**A rare aerial view of the yard, taken in 1932, showing the engine shed and coaling stage to the left, and the wagon repair shop to the right. In the background is Hanworth Air Park with what is believed to be the airship *Graf Zeppelin* on view.**

**Above:**
An unusual experiment in early floodlighting. An old barrage balloon was used to suspend an 8ft ring carrying 20 1,000-watt lamps, 10 of which had 19in reflectors, suspended 150ft above the yard. The balloon was mounted on to a wagon enabling it to be moved to various parts of the yard. The experiment proved a success and led to the installation of permanent floodlighting.

**Below:**
The engine shed could accommodate 42 engines with tenders. To the right is the coaling stage with its 12,000-ton capacity.  Ian Allan Library

**Bottom:**
Seen here is the west end of the yard, 'S15' 4-6-0 No 30499 leaves with a down freight, whilst diesel shunter No 13042 waits in the siding. Ian Allan Library

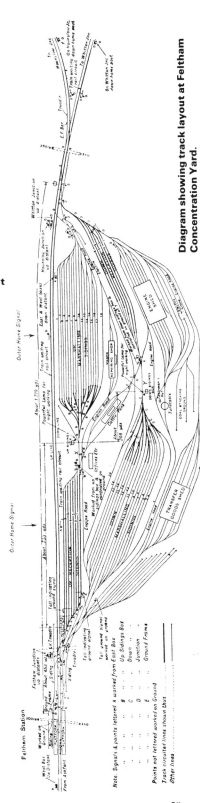

**Diagram showing track layout at Feltham Concentration Yard.**

Top:
**A down goods from Feltham approaches the main line at West Weybridge, behind 'S15' 4-6-0 No 30500 in June 1955.**  J. F. Hemmings

Above:
**An up freight for Feltham crosses Thorpe Lane between Egham and Staines, hauled by 'H16' 4-6-2T No 30517 in May 1952. Five of these engines were built in 1921 by Urie for interchange workings between Brent sidings, on the Midland Railway, Willesden on the LNWR and Feltham yard.**  D. Sutton Collection

The Southern Years

Whitchurch

# The South Western Heritage

It took some years after 1 January 1923 to accept Waterloo as the terminus of the South Western Section of the Southern Railway. An official reminder that this was the case was published in 1925, at which time official ears were displeased to hear the terms South Western, the Brighton and South Eastern still being used, kept alive by their frequent appearance in the newspapers. It is said that one South Western official at Clapham Junction would refer to his Brighton neighbour as 'the Hornby railway next door'.

Solid reminders of the South Western remained all over the system. In distant Cornwall three 2-4-0 well tanks of the design first built in the days of Joseph Beattie were still at work on the Bodmin & Wadebridge line. They no longer had the chocolate-colour livery and tall polished brass dome cover, towering above the weatherboard that was the driver's only protection, with which the originals were launched, and they had been built after Joseph had been succeeded by his son, W. G. Beattie, but as 'Beattie well tanks' they kept a famous name alive.

Joseph Beattie put the London & South Western on the technical map by his interest in fuel efficiency. His experiments with burning coal without smoke led to some unusual firebox arrangements which in time gave place to a simpler system, but his feedwater heater in its final form earned a high reputation for extracting the utmost energy from the fuel. W. G. Beattie was only in charge of locomotives for six years after his father's death in 1871. For the most part he continued with the designs of his father's period and the Bodmin & Wadebridge well tanks inherited by the Southern Railway had actually been built by Beyer Peacock while Joseph was in charge. He also took a step forward by designing his own type of piston valve which he incorporated in a 4-4-0 express locomotive with outside cylinders. In service the piston valves proved to have some inherent design weaknesses. The engines were a disappointment, in particular it seems to Beattie himself, for he resigned in the year after they appeared. His successor, William Adams, did what he could for them, beginning by replacing the valves, but the class was finally withdrawn in 1905.

The Adams imprint on the Southern Railway was still strong. Seventeen of his classes were taken over. His mixed traffic and tank engines abounded, the most numerous class in 1923 being the 0-4-2 'Jubilees' with all 90 representatives still in action. Perhaps, when watching the 'Hornby railway next door', Adams had been impressed by

Running via West Moors and the Avon Valley line, this Salisbury-Bournemouth train is seen between Salisbury and Alderbury Junction, hauled by an ex-LSWR 'T3' class No E558. The prefix 'E' to the number indicates that the locomotive was an ex-LSWR engine.   L&GRP (11230)

Right:
**Emerging from Honiton Tunnel, 'T9' 4-4-0 No 286 heads a down train for Exeter. This 1,345yd tunnel was one of the LSWR's greatest feats of civil engineering.**
Ian Allan Library

Stroudley's 'Gladstones'. His choice of a front-coupled design for a tender engine is surprising, for his distinctive contribution to locomotive engineering was the Adams four-wheel bogie with a pivot which was allowed controlled sideplay and made for smooth negotiation of curves by locomotives with coupled wheels.

Early in his period of office Adams had some 4-4-0 tank engines built to help out with a growing suburban traffic that was getting beyond the older classes. In this series the livery was changed to a dark umber similar to that of the Brighton engines. Later he rebuilt the class with a trailing radial axle. Some of the rebuilds lasted until 1925. More 4-4-2 tank engines followed at the beginning of the 1880s. They flourished in the London area until electrification displaced them, when most of them went to the West Country. Three worked on the Lyme Regis branch right into the British Railways years and one of the three can still be seen in steam on the Bluebell Railway. For main line work a number of 4-4-0s were built, all with outside cylinders and some with 7ft 1in driving wheels. Their appearance was elegant rather than robust but they were capable of excellent work. In the middle 1880s Adams changed the livery of goods engines and the older classes to a dark 'holly' green, but all new passenger engines including some Beattie rebuilds were painted a light pea green with black and white lining.

Nineteenth century locomotive engineers are sometimes given less credit than they deserve for their efforts to improve the efficiency of their engines. In retrospect, performance is more exciting than pounds, shillings and pence, but the engineers had to produce figures of coal and oil costs with a ratio to work done that would satisfy the boardroom. Adams attempted to make the steam work harder by an experiment in compounding. Trials of a Webb compound loaned by

the London & North Western Railway on the Waterloo-Exeter service showed no advantage over the South Western simples, but Adams persisted and converted his 7ft 1in 4-4-0 No 446 into a compound on the Worsdell-von Borries system by replacing one 'live steam' cylinder with a low-pressure cylinder of 26in diameter in which the steam did further work before being exhausted to atmosphere. The experiment was begun in 1881 and No 446 ran as a compound for three years before being restored to simple propulsion.

The strongest South Western imprint on the motive power of the new Southern Railway in 1923 was left by Dugald Drummond, who succeeded Adams in 1895. On the eve of Grouping, 371 of his engines were in service out of a total South Western stock of 911. Drummond came from the Caledonian Railway, bringing with him a tradition of sturdy 4-4-0 main line locomotives with inside cylinders. His first products at Nine Elms, however, were the 0-4-4 tank engines remembered today as the 'M7' class. Appearing in 1897, they worked at first west of Exeter but later took over most of the suburban traffic and numerous semi-fast workings. Some had a conical smokebox door to allow room for a rather complicated spark-arresting arrangement. Also in 1897 the first deliveries were received from Dübs & Company of the 0-6-0 goods engines which became known as 'Black Motors'. Many South Western engines were built by outside firms to the company's designs (sometimes the firms had a considerable influence on the finished product). From 1874 to 1887 no locomotives had been built at Nine Elms. Over that period the works confined itself to rebuilding older types and general repairs.

Drummond's first express locomotive was completed at Nine Elms in 1897. It was a four-cylinder machine with inside cylinders driving the leading axle and an outside pair, set behind the

bogie, driving a second axle. The two driven axles were uncoupled, so that the engine was a 'double single' or 4-2-2-0. A similar arrangement in some of Francis Webb's locomotives for the LNWR had adhesion problems at starting but they were compounds and Drummond may have hoped that this accounted for their peculiarities. The 11ft spacing of the driving axles allowed a very long firebox but the 27½sq ft of grate area and 1,664sq ft total heating surface did not meet the demands of the 16½in dia and 26in stroke cylinders and they were soon fitted with liners to reduce the diameter to 14in. Five more 'double singles' were built at Nine Elms in 1901 and all came into Southern Railway ownership but did not last long. No 720, the pioneer of this unsatisfactory experiment, was given a larger boiler in 1905 and ran until 1927. The boiler was finally used for carriage heating at Clapham. No 720 introduced the tender with two four-wheel bogies and inside bearings to all axles which later became a Drummond characteristic. It also had the first Drummond cross-tube firebox which increased the heating surface with a number of water tubes at right angles to the length of the box. By bringing water into the hottest part of the firebox, this arrangement increased the circulation and improved steaming. All six 'double singles' came into Southern Railway ownership but were withdrawn during the 1920s. No 720, the original, was given a larger boiler and was in service until 1927, after which its boiler was piped for steam-heating coaches at Clapham.

After this experiment in express locomotive design Drummond reverted to the classic 4-4-0 with inside cylinders for which he is best remembered. There were several classes, all taken over by the Southern Railway. The first of his celebrated 'T9' 4-4-0s were built at Nine Elms and by Dübs & Co in 1899-1900. The Dübs engines had cross-tube fireboxes which gave them another 165sq ft of heating surface. In their original form the 'T9s' clearly showed Drummond's Caledonian background. Rebuilding and superheating in later years gave them a leaner look more in keeping with their name of 'Greyhounds', in itself a tribute to a dashing performance.

In the early years of the century the 4-6-0 was beginning to take its place as an express locomotive. Drummond turned to this type with a four-cylinder design in 1905, by which time the Great Western had been turning out the 4-6-0 'Saints' for two years. Drummond's designs were less successful and there was a good deal of double-heading by 'T9s' on heavy trains. The best of his 4-6-0s were the 'T14' class, known as 'Paddleboxes'. This is supposed to have been because their deep splashers were reminiscent of the paddleboxes on the steamers that ran short sea trips from the resorts served by the railway. In fact, the slotted spashers of the Beattie days were closer in appearance and it has been suggested that the name was given many years before to a Joseph Beattie design with valves on top of the outside cylinders and visible above the platform. The 'T14' valves were similarly placed. Whatever their performance may have been, all Drummond's 4-6-0s were impressive to look at. This aspect was enhanced in the 'T14s' by a 5,800gal eight-wheel tender in their later years.

Drummond's engines were not superheated but in the later 'T14s' he used a device called a steam drier. It consisted of a chamber in the smokebox containing a number of 2in dia tubes through which hot gases flowed from the boiler flue tubes. Steam entering the chamber was directed by baffles and then flowed upwards over the hot tubes to the steampipe connection to the cylinders at the top of the chamber. On its passage through the drier the steam reached a temperature of about 400°F.

Drummond died in 1912 while still in office, at the age of 72. R. W. Urie who followed him had been his works manager and had previously worked under him as Chief Draughtsman on the Caledonian Railway. Urie first turned his attention to superheating and rebuilding but he had produced a new 4-6-0 mixed traffic design before World War 1 severely curtailed new construction. These 'H15' class engines, with two outside cylinders and 6ft wheels, struck a new note for the South Western with their Walschaerts valve gear, high running plates and outside bearings for the tender bogie axles. After the war Urie went further along the same lines with his 'N15' express passenger 4-6-0 with 6ft 7in wheels. This time a short semi-stovepipe chimney seemed to accentuate the size of the boiler. The writer first saw an 'N15' from the platform at Honiton station as it bore down upon him with the train that was to convey him to Templecombe, and he was awestruck, being used to taper boilers and the decorative flourish of copper chimney caps on the Great Western. The 'N15s' were the most significant legacy of the South Western to the Southern, for they were the inspiration for the 'King Arthur' class and were incorporated into it. A version for main line freight traffic, with 6ft wheels (the 'S15' class), was introduced by Urie and also built by the Southern Railway.

Urie's last two classes were both associated with the great marshalling yard at Feltham, completed in 1922. A 4-6-2T ('H16' class) was built for transfer traffic. Passengers to and from St Pancras

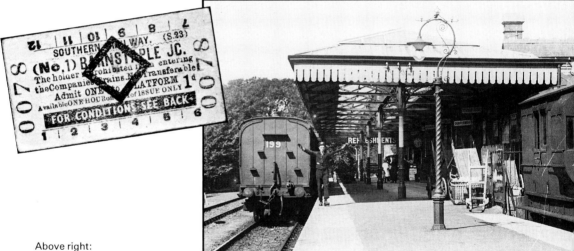

**Above right:**
**Today there is no trace of Bude station, but in this 1923 view, two-coach set No 199 stands in the platform as the motive power backs on and passengers say their farewells.** L&GRP (8871)

**Right:**
**The Friary station at Plymouth was the LSWR's most westerly main line terminus. Seen here in 1935 a 'T9' heads a train for Exeter and Waterloo. Plymouth Friary closed in 1958 and from then on all Southern Region trains terminated at the former joint station at Plymouth North Road.** L&GRP (11250)

would often catch a glimpse of Southern green as they passed Cricklewood, for these engines were painted in the passenger colour. Hump shunting in the yard was undertaken by four 'G16' 4-8-0Ts.

The traditions of a railway are to be seen in its passenger rolling stock as well as in its locomotives. The most recent South Western passenger stock at Grouping were some five-coach corridor sets built in 1921 for the Bournemouth service. The designer was Surrey Warner, who from the time he took office as Carriage & Wagon Superintendent in 1906 had been building up the South Western's previously sparse supply of corridor stock so that the number of restaurant car trains could be increased. This much improved the South Western's image in comparison with the other southern lines. Warner's predecessor, W. Panter, had begun the move by adapting some centre-corridor saloons in 1901. They had been built for the 'American Eagle Express' between Waterloo and Southampton when transatlantic liners began calling at the port from 1896, but at first were not used as dining cars because the journey was thought too short to create a demand for meals en route. There had been a short experiment with a borrowed Pullman car on the West of England line in 1877, and from 1890 four Pullman cars worked on Bournemouth trains but passengers soon deserted them for restaurant cars when these became available. Warner's first cars were dignified with the name 'Dining Saloon' but the impression of spaciousness was misleading. Only 28 passengers could be seated and the overflow had to be served with meals on tables fitted up in the compartments of adjoining coaches.

In the Bournemouth sets of 1921 there was a pantry compartment in one Third Class coach from which teas and light refreshments could be served to passengers in the other compartments of the set. This arrangement was described officially as 'an alternative to the conventional tea basket' on services which did not call for full restaurant cars. The boiler in the pantry was 'of a capacity sufficient to supply tea to all passengers'. There was also an egg cooker and a grill. The coaches had external steel panelling although the body framework was still timber. Warships were in the news in those days and so they became known as 'Ironclads'. Construction was continued by the Southern Railway. With hindsight, the 'Ironclads' can be regarded as forerunners of the 6-PAN sets of the Eastbourne electrification. It may also be noted that when Churchward built some massive restaurant cars for the Great Western in 1904 they were dubbed 'Dreadnoughts'.

The main line passenger livery of the South Western was distinctive. Below the waist line the colour was dark brown. Above the waist it has been variously described, often as 'salmon pink' but this shade came with age and weathering. When first out of the shops it has been described by C. Hamilton Ellis — an artist both with words and the brush — as 'a beautiful golden brown, like the cliffs at Bournemouth . . .'. The electric trains first made dark green familiar on passenger stock. It did not reach the main line coaches until 1920.

Other South Western features were a useful legacy to the Southern. The railway had been a pioneer of automatic signalling with a low-pressure electro-pneumatic system controlled through the track circuits. When installed between Andover and Grateley in 1902 it was the first automatic semaphore signalling on a British main line. This installation was removed during World War 1 when a junction for military traffic was put in, but the system lasted on the main line between Woking and Basingstoke until it was resignalled with colour lights for the Bournemouth electrification of 1967.

The gantries carrying signal posts, each with a stop and distant arm, were a distinctive feature of the Woking-Basingstoke section. With a track circuit unoccupied the track relay was energised and through its contacts passed current to a magnet valve which admitted air to a cylinder and lowered the stop arm of the relevant signal. If the signal ahead was 'off' a contact on the stop arm completed a circuit to lower the distant arm as well. When a train passed the signal and occupied the track circuit the track relay was de-energised and the air supply to the stop arm cylinder was cut off. On returning to 'danger' the arm broke the circuit to the distant arm valve. With its air supply cut off, the distant arm returned to 'caution'.

At Waterloo the 'A' signalbox had grown over the years. Its last renewal before Grouping had been in 1892. It then had three lever frames with 75, 159 and 75 levers and was not replaced by an all-electric box until 1936.

All sections of the Southern Railway benefited from the South Western's quarries at Meldon, at the foot of Yes Tor on Dartmoor. A district engineer on the railway in the 1890s found that Dartmoor rock made good ballast for the permanent way. At first he chipped it out of the sides of cuttings but in 1897 the railway began quarrying operations at a rock face. The stone was obtained by blasting and then crushed before being loaded into hopper wagons for conveyance all over the system. In years to come the quarry stone would be supplied to the whole of the Southern Railway. By the 1930s eight or nine ballast trains each of 10 40-ton hopper wagons were being despatched from the quarries every week. The first wagons were built by Surrey Warner and their successors remained virtually unchanged from his design.

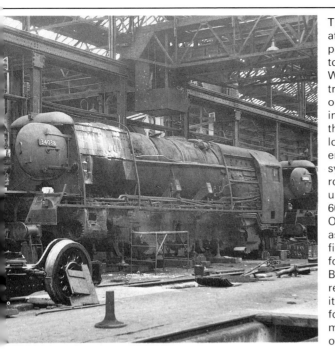

Left:
**Wheeling a Urie 4-6-0, using the two 50-ton Vaughan cranes in the erecting shop in 1939.**
Ian Allan Library

Above:
**West Country class No 34038 *Lynton* undergoes major overhaul in the workshops in July 1953.**
Ian Allan Library

Below:
**After the Grouping in 1923, the C&W works began building rolling stock for other areas of the Southern, here in 1932 seat testing takes place alongside the construction of coaches for the new electric services on the Brighton line.**
Ian Allan Library

The LSWR began producing locomotives in 1843, at their works situated next to the original passenger and goods terminus at Nine Elms. Due to an increase in freight traffic the Locomotive Works along with the running shed were transferred in 1865 to a new 23-acre site on the opposite side of the main line, which also included a new Carriage & Wagon Works. By now the company had the capacity to build up to 20 locomotives and tenders per year. Towards the end of the 19th century, the rapid growth of the system led to a need for more locomotives and rolling stock. In particular the C&W Works was unable to construct new rolling stock more than 60ft long over buffers, due to the lack of room. Over the years the works had expanded as much as space would allow, so the Directors decided to find another location. Two suitable sites were found — one at Andover, the other at Eastleigh. Both were in a central location where land was relatively cheap. Eastleigh was the final choice as it had easy access to Portsmouth and Salisbury for the West of England, besides being on the main line to Bournemouth and within a few miles of Southampton Docks. The C&W Works moved to their new site situated to the north of the Portsmouth line opposite Eastleigh station in 1890. These new works were now able to build coaches equal in comfort and looks to those of any other railway company, from the luxury family carriage or restaurant cars, to carriages that formed the majority of ordinary trains.

On 31 December 1909 the Locomotive Works also transferred to Eastleigh, located in the angle that forms the junction of the main and Portsmouth lines. The last engine to be built at Nine Elms was 'B4' dock tank No 84, which entered service in June 1908; the first to be built at the new works was a motor tank No 101, built on 12 September 1910. The new Locomotive Works was spacious and well-lit and at that time was the most advanced in the country, and was now able to produce all of the locomotive requirements for the company. Throughout its life the works was well maintained, keeping it in line with all the modern practices, both under the Southern Railway and British Railways. Between 1910 and 1961 a total of 425 locomotives had either been built or rebuilt at the works. The last engine to be built at Eastleigh was a Bulleid 'West Country' class Pacific No 34104 *Bere Alston* in April 1950, and by coincidence it was also the last to be rebuilt in May 1961. The last steam locomotive to be officially repaired was a 'Battle of Britain' class No 34089, *602 Squadron*, outshopped on 3 October 1966. In 1958 work began on provisions for a diesel repair shop, which was completed by June 1959. During the early 1960s a nationwide programme of rationalisation of BR's workshops took place, and by 1967 the C&W Works had been moved to an already much reduced Locomotive Works. Eastleigh Works played an important role in the economy of the area.

# The 'Arthurs' and After

R. E. L. Maunsell, the first Chief Mechanical Engineer of the Southern Railway, was a South Eastern man. His most celebrated contribution to Western Section motive power was his continuation and improvement of Urie's 'N15' 4-6-0s to form the 'King Arthur' class. He modified the valve gear and blast arrangements of the existing engines and put in hand new construction on the same principles at Eastleigh and with the North British Locomotive Co. There were, therefore, three categories of 'King Arthurs': the modified Urie engines, the new engines from Eastleigh, and the new engines built by North British (the 'Scotch Arthurs'). The name for the class was suggested by John (later Sir John) Elliot, at that time Assistant to the General Manager for Advertising & Publicity. The new engines were named after the Knights of the Round Table while the updated Urie engines were named after other characters and places in the Arthurian legend.

Elliot's choice of name for the class is generally acknowledged as a public relations masterstroke for the reputation of the railway was suffering in the difficult postwar years. The press made little allowance for the problems of working a complex railway system around London with material that was often ageing and inadequate, and suffering from restricted maintenance during the war years. King Arthur had swept his country clear of enemies, and the 'King Arthur' locomotives seemed to embody a similar fighting spirit in the face of hostile comment, with an assurance of success. The names were also a reminder of the distant horizons of the Southern Railway to those who perhaps had thought of it in terms of short journeys to the coastal resorts nearer London. In the mind's eye the 'Arthurs' were always seen as

DORSET SERVED BY BRITISH RAILWAYS

racing westwards towards King Arthur's court at Camelot.

Two Maunsell classes which became familiar on the Western Section had their origin in the requirements of the former South Eastern lines. The 'Lord Nelson' 4-6-0s of 1926 were built for working the increasingly heavy Continental boat trains, and the 'Schools' 4-4-0s had to meet the growing demands of expresses on the Tonbridge-Hastings line. In the 'Nelsons' the Southern Railway briefly possessed the 'most powerful' British express locomotive, the nominal tractive effort being 33.500lb. Publicity material tended to ignore the word 'nominal' and did not dwell on the fact that power and tractive effort are not interchangeable terms. This was a four-cylinder locomotive with the cranks set to give eight beats per revolution to provide a uniform torque and steady draught. On the Western Section they worked on the Bournemouth line, particularly with the 'Bournemouth Belle' Pullman, and took West of England trains between Waterloo and Salisbury (for a time in their early days they worked to and from Exeter). When the 'Bournemouth Limited' two-hour non-stop service was inaugurated in July 1929, No 860 *Lord Hawke* made a demonstration run on 4 July with a 13-coach train and reached Bournemouth 1¼min inside schedule. It was reported that 'the finest running was done after New Milton, 85mph being attained between Hinton Admiral and Christ-church'.

In designing the 'Schools' for the Hastings line, Maunsell had to allow for the restricted loading gauge which prevented the use of two outside cylinders of adequate power. He therefore produced a three-cylinder engine with a 4-4-0 wheel arrangement. The adhesion of a six-coupled design would have been useful but curvature and the size of existing turntables restricted the length. The capability of the 'Schools', in spite of the limitations imposed by the route for which they were designed, has earned them the title of 'Maunsell's masterpiece'. On the Western Section they first earned their laurels on the Portsmouth Direct line and when that line was electrified in 1937 went on to a distinguished career on the Bournemouth service.

Electrification of the Brighton line brought an 'import' to the Western Section. There was now little work for the LBSCR 4-6-4 tank engines and in 1934 Maunsell rebuilt them as 4-6-0 tender engines, increasing the boiler pressure to 180lb/

sq in and making them generally equivalent to the 'King Arthurs'. They were classified 'N15X'. As rebuilt with a shorter chimney and side window cab they could be used on all Southern main lines except Tonbridge-Hastings. The name of the ex-LBSCR war memorial engine, *Remembrance*, was retained but the other six engines were named after engineers.

O. V. S. Bulleid took over from Maunsell in 1937 and, like Maunsell, in his early days he had to look for greater power from the locomotives. At first he set about improving the performance of the 'Nelsons' by modifying the exhaust arrangements, continuing a process begun by Maunsell when he equipped No 862 *Lord Collingwood* with two Kylchap blastpipes and a double chimney. Bulleid also began fitting Lemaître blastpipes and large-diameter chimneys to 'Schools' class locomotives, but his ultimate objective was a Pacific. When war broke out in 1939 the building of new express engines had to stop. Bulleid's Pacific design had 6ft 2in wheels and qualified as a mixed traffic locomotive. Construction was sanctioned and the first 'Merchant Navy' Pacific came out in 1941. An 'air-smoothed' exterior and an individualistic style of numbering caused considerable comment but the most discussed feature was the valve gear. It was a three-cylinder engine with the valve gear for all cylinders between the frames. Since there was no room for the orthodox connections from the crank axle to the three sets of gear there was a double chain drive from the axle to a layshaft, and from the layshaft to a three-throw crankshaft for operating the valves. The mechanism was enclosed in a casing with an oil sump in the bottom. Gear-type pumps in the sump fed oil to the moving parts. Experience with the locomotives in service revealed a tendency to leakage from the sump and poor control of the valve events. In spite of this Bulleid retained the same arrangements in his light 'West Country' Pacifics after the war. Under British Railways, however, the 'Merchant Navys' and a number of 'West Countrys' were rebuilt with conventional Walschaerts valve gear. The 'air-smoothed' casing was removed. In their new form the locomotives gave excellent service and met British Rail criteria for accessibility and easy servicing.

Before retirement Maunsell had designed the 'Q' class 0-6-0 with an 18-ton axleload giving it a wide route availability. These engines took over the work of some of the ageing pre-Grouping freight locomotives. The first of them came out after Bulleid had taken command. When wartime traffic called for more locomotives of a similar type, Bulleid introduced his own 'Q1' 0-6-0, an 'Austerity' design stamped with its author's individualistic ideas but winning few friends for its appearance.

Left:

**A down Weymouth Express is seen near Moreton, hauled by 'King Arthur' 4-6-0 No 783** *Sir Gillemere* **in 1935.** L&GRP (345)

Below:
**A period piece, long before the introduction of the 'ACE', the 11am departure for Plymouth stands at the main line Platform 1 at Waterloo.**
British Railways

**The unique 'T7' 4-2-2-0 No 720 heads the 11am West of England express through Earlsfield in 1911.** Real Photographs (T6138)

IM TAKING AN
EARLY HOLIDAY COS
i KNOW SUMMER
COMES SOONEST IN THE SOUTH
SOUTHERN RAILWAY

For many years the LSWR timetable advertised an 11am West of England express, but it was not until 1926 that the SR gave this slot to the most famous train to run over the old LSWR metals, the 'Atlantic Coast Express', or the 'ACE' as it was sometimes called. The 'ACE' had the distinction of being the most multi-portioned train in the country, there being nine in total. At the leading end of the train there was an Ilfracombe section consisting of two brake thirds with a composite coach between. This was followed by brake composites each for Torrington, Padstow, Bude and Plymouth, after which came two restaurant cars which were detached at Exeter Central. Behind these followed brake composites for Exmouth, Sidmouth and a Seaton coach detached at Salisbury — the latter calling at all stations to Seaton. The 'ACE' ran non-stop between Waterloo and Salisbury, then again non-stop to Sidmouth Junction where the Sidmouth and Exmouth coaches came off and then worked together to Tipton St Johns where they were divided. In 1939 the 'ACE' covered the 171.75 miles from Waterloo to Exeter Central in 3hr 12min. Here a general break-up of the train occurred. The restaurant cars were detached and the remaining coaches divided in two. The first off were the Ilfracombe and Torrington portions booked to leave Central station at 2.18pm taking 62min to Barnstaple Junction where the Torrington coach was detached and a through coach from the 'Cornish Riviera Ltd', which came via the GWR line from Taunton, was attached to the Ilfracombe section. The 226.5-mile journey to Ilfracombe was completed at 4.06pm — 8min after the Torrington coach reached its destination. The three remaining portions left at Exeter Central were booked to leave at 2.23pm for Okehampton, usually with three extra coaches attached to the Plymouth section. At Okehampton the Padstow and Bude coaches were detached and ran together as far as Halwill Junction. Bude was reached at 4.39pm and Padstow, 275.75 miles from Waterloo, was reached at 5.37pm, making this the longest through working on the SR. The Plymouth portion arrived at the Friary terminus at 4.19pm. In the height of the summer season the 'ACE' ran as two services; the Ilfracombe, Torrington, Bude and Padstow portions left Waterloo at 10.35am, the Sidmouth, Exmouth and Plymouth portions departing at 11am. On summer Saturdays there were no fewer than eight separate restaurant car trains required, departing between 10.24am and 12.05pm, while in the up direction a similar pattern followed.

Left:
**Before the introduction of Bulleid's Pacifics, 'King Arthur' 4-6-0s were usually put in charge of the 'ACE'. Here, No 456 *Sir Galahad* speeds through Milborne Port in 1935.** L&GRP (356)

Throughout the life of the train many improvements were made to timings and speeds. In 1952 the 'ACE' was booked to arrive at Exeter at 2.06pm, beating the 11am departure from Paddington by a clear half-hour. The best and final improvement came in October 1961, when the 83.8 miles to Salisbury was covered in 80min and Exeter was reached in 2hr 56min, 2hr 58min being allowed for the up working. From then on the 'ACE' was reaching the end of its long and distinguished history. In 1963 the old enemy at Paddington took over all SR lines west of Wilton and set to replacing Southern steam with Western diesels to the west of Salisbury and terminating all Waterloo trains at Exeter. From 4 September 1964 the 'Atlantic Coast Express' was no more.

Above left:
**Carrying its headboard, the up 'ACE' passes to the east of Yeovil Junction behind 'Merchant Navy' Pacific No 35021 *New Zealand Line* in 1950.**
L&GRP (23382)

Left:
**Arriving at Okehampton behind 'West Country' Pacific No 34030 *Watersmeet* in October 1949, the 'ACE' will leave the North Cornwall sections behind, before continuing on to Plymouth.**
Real Photographs (K481)

Above:
**In its final years, the 'ACE' approaches Clapham Junction in May 1961 behind rebuilt 'Merchant Navy' Pacific No 35019 *French Line CGT*.**
G. F. Heiron

# The Southern Imprint

The designer of passenger coaches has to gauge public reactions. His products have a role in marketing the railway. Maunsell had a mixed bag of coaching stock on his hands and soon set about establishing a recognisable Southern type. In 1925 he ordered a standard design of 59ft corridor vehicles including six First Class kitchen/restaurant cars and six Third Class cars (without kitchen). There could be an end now to the practice of putting up tables in compartments, for the Third Class cars enabled 64 passengers to be served in a centre-gangway saloon. The 'Bournemouth Limited' train of 1929, which revived a prewar two-hour Waterloo-Bournemouth schedule, was formed of the new Southern stock. It had at first a fixed formation of 10 vehicles. Four coaches which came off at Bournemouth carried 'Bournemouth Limited' roofboards; four coaches (including the restaurant car) were labelled for Bournemouth and Weymouth; and two more carried Wareham and Swanage destination boards. *The Railway Gazette* explained that 'by adopting a "limited"

make-up it is hoped to achieve punctual running under all reasonable circumstances. Prewar trains could not always run to time when heavily loaded. The train will of course be worked by "King Arthur" or "Lord Nelson" engines'.

In later years the 'limited' formation was increased to 11 vehicles, and when Bulleid succeeded Maunsell he refurbished some 11-coach sets for this service, painting them malachite green. Seven 'Schools' class locomotives were given a matching livery. When these changes were introduced in 1938 *The Railway Gazette* said of the trains: 'Externally they are painted a plain unlined bright green, and headed by one of the handsome and efficient "Schools" class engines similarly coloured but with conventional black and white lining present a very striking appearance . . . Truly Mr Bulleid is to be congratulated on his first effort in cheering the passenger by congenial surroundings.' Bulleid's efforts had, indeed, extended to new internal colour schemes, individual seat backs in all compartments, and framed paintings replacing maps and advertisements in the thirds. Malachite, it may be added, is a green mineral. Malachite green is defined as a colour produced by a dye of the triphenylmethane series (which may not convey much to those who have not seen it).

Pullman cars returned to the Bournemouth service when the 'Bournemouth Belle' was put on in 1931. The LBSCR having made the 'Southern Belle' title very much its own, the Southern

*Below:*
**A rebuilt 'N15X' Class No 2332 *Stroudley* speeds a down West of England express under the much photographed Battledown Flyover near Basingstoke, carrying the up Southampton main line over the main line to Salisbury, in 1938.**
L&GRP (6638)

Railway was obliged to adopt names for its Pullman trains which still bring an echo of seaside pleasure steamers. Brief histories of the 'Bournemouth Belle' and other named trains on the Western Section are included in this publication.

Electrification made up a large part of the Southern image between the wars. It was the age of 'Southern Electric' signs directing travellers to stations where, in accordance with Sir Herbert Walker's precepts, they would be sure of catching a train without a long wait. He thought 15min quite long enough. On the Western Section the electrification from Raynes Park to Dorking North in 1925 brought services from Waterloo to Dorking, previously a LBSCR preserve. At the same time the Guildford via Cobham electrification, which had stopped at Claygate during the war, was extended to Guildford and the line from Leatherhead which joined it at Effingham Junction was also electrified. One station at Leatherhead replaced the previous separate LBSCR and LSWR establishments. Rationalisation at Epsom followed. Originally LBSCR trains for Dorking and beyond called at their own station in Epsom and ran through the LSWR's Epsom station on the centre tracks. A new Epsom station with platforms for Western and Central Section trains was opened on the former LSWR site on 3 March 1929 and the LBSCR station (named Epsom Town by the Southern Railway) was closed.

On the Windsor Lines electrification was extended from junctions with the Hounslow loop to Staines and Windsor on 6 July 1930. Staines to Virginia Water and the main line at Weybridge followed on 3 January 1937. This was a key year in Western Section electrification for it saw completion of the Portsmouth No 1 scheme. The work involved extending electrification along the main line from Hampton Court Junction to Woking, and over the Portsmouth Direct line to Guildford, Havant and Portsmouth. Waterloo-Portsmouth electric services began on 4 July 1937.

Before electrification the Southern Railway had revitalised a rather flagging Portsmouth service by introducing some non-stop trains which made the journey in 98min, improving on the previous fastest by 16min. With its severe gradients the route was a hard one for steam locomotives. For a

Below:
**An up mixed train hauled by Adams '415' No 3125 is seen to the east of Combpyne on the Lyme Regis branch in April 1939. The small wagon behind the engine is an old LSWR road van, with sliding doors for parcels collection. Eventually, the SR added the prefix '3' to all ex-South Western locomotives on the duplicate list.**   L&GPR (2029)

**ELECTRIFICATION!**

**700 MILES OF SOUTHERN RAIL-
WAY WILL BE ELECTRIFIED BY
SPRING NEXT YEAR ~ 3 NEW
SECTIONS OPEN THIS SUMMER
~ 3 ELECTRIC FOR EVERY STEAM
TRAIN NOW RUNNING ~ ~ ~
~ TOTAL COST £8,000,000**

**WORLD'S GREATEST SUBURBAN
ELECTRIC**

**SOUTHERN**

Top:
**A second programme of electrification took place
during 1937, covering all outer suburban routes
including the Portsmouth line. Here, 2-NOL EMU
No 1872 rounds the tight curve into Chertsey
station, on the Virginia Water-Weybridge branch.**
British Railways

long time Drummond 'D15' 4-4-0s were the most
successful performers on the Portsmouth trains but
when 'Schools' came to the service in 1935 the best
non-stop time was brought down to 90min. On
electrification the same time was achieved by the
hourly fast trains with stops at Guildford and
Haslemere. At the same time as the line to
Portsmouth was electrified the third rail was
extended along the main line to Pirbright Junction
and over the branch to Alton.

The new express electric trains for the
Portsmouth service were four-car units with
corridor connections at both ends so that when two
or more units were coupled together passengers
could walk from one end of the train to the other
and all had access to the restaurant car. An electric
train with a blanked-off corridor connection
leading was something not seen before. The
driver's window was on one side of the connection
and the route indicator on the other. This
arrangement was considered to give the trains a
one-eyed appearance and suggested the nickname
'Nelsons' which at least was appropriate to their
naval associations.

The units were classified 4-COR, or 4-RES if
with a restaurant car. A 4-COR set consisted of an
open third motorcoach at each end with a
compartment composite and a compartment third
between. In the 4-RES sets the trailers were a First
Class car with four compartments and an open
dining saloon, and a Third Class car with kitchen,
pantry and open dining section.

The two motorcoaches in a set were each
powered by two 225hp motors in one bogie. At
that time most traction motors were totally
enclosed because of misgivings over dirt and dust
being deposited on the machines by cooling air
drawn in from outside. The frames of the
Portsmouth motors were finned to increase the
area for heat dissipation and keep the temperature
rise on the long gradients of the Portsmouth line

within acceptable limits. Doubts may have been expressed in high places whether 900hp was adequate for a four-car set for Charles Klapper related in *Sir Herbert Walker's Southern Railway* how Alfred Raworth, the Chief Electrical Engineer, murmured a reassuring 'these motors are just right' on several occasions during a demonstration run.

With the creation of the Southern Railway the LBSCR Portsmouth route from Victoria had become secondary, the traffic being concentrated at Waterloo. As part of the breakdown of inter-Section barriers, however, good use was made of the Central Section line from Dorking to Horsham and Portsmouth via Ford by weekend 'extras' from Waterloo which took the Epsom branch at Raynes Park. A year after Portsmouth No 1 the Central Section route was electrified in the Portsmouth No 2 scheme. Electric traction was already in use to Dorking. It was now extended to Horsham and over the Mid-Sussex line (today called the Arun Valley Line) to Ford. Simultaneous electrification from West Worthing to Havant closed the gap between Ford and Portsmouth No 1 so that Portsmouth electrics from Waterloo could again travel via Dorking if necessary.

In the last Western Section electrification before World War 2 the system was extended from Virginia Water to Reading (43½ miles from Waterloo) and over lines in the Ascot/Aldershot area which provided an all-electric route from Ascot to Guildford (with reversal at Aldershot). With these additions the extent of the Southern Electric system was 655 route miles.

The Western Section also acquired some new lines in Southern Railway days. As mentioned earlier, the Halwill Junction-Torrington line had its origins before World War 1 although it was not completed and opened until 27 July 1925, when the Southern Railway leased it from the North Devon & Cornwall Railway Company. Halwill Junction

was 600ft above sea level and there was a drop of 523ft to Torrington, but with some sharp undulations during the descent. The summit of a ridge between Hatherleigh and Meeth had to be crossed with climbs at 1 in 38/42 in both directions. There was a drop at 1 in 50 approaching Torrington.

Far removed in distance and environment from this country railway was the Wimbledon & Sutton line in the outer London suburbs. The project had originated in 1910 but was dormant until revived by the Southern Railway in 1923 as a countermove to a proposed extension of the City & South London line. Agreement was reached that the Southern should build the Wimbledon & Sutton and that the tube should stop at Morden. Construction of the line, which was electrified from the outset, began in 1927 and it was opened to a junction with the Central Section at Sutton on 5 January 1930. Surprisingly in view of its situation, the line was steeply graded, nearly matching Halwill Junction-Torrington in some places such as 1 in 49/44 approaching Sutton and 1 in 60 elsewhere.

At Wimbledon there was a junction with a line to Tooting and Streatham which had been opened on 1 October 1868. This had been promoted by an independent Wimbledon, Merton & Tooting company but its powers to build the line were transferred jointly to the LBSCR and the LSWR. In 1878 the LBSCR bought the South Western's interest in the line, which became LBSCR property. It was electrified on 3 March 1929 so that trains from the Wimbledon & Sutton were able to run through to London Bridge.

Another LBSCR/LSWR joint line at Wimbledon was from West Croydon. It was electrified on 6 July 1930. Fears of closure have arisen from time to time in recent years, but at the time of writing (1987) its two-car sets continue to ply over a route that is largely single-track.

The Wimbledon-Streatham line briefly carried a main line service in 1939. Imperial Airways, operator of the Empire Air routes, had built a terminal adjacent to Victoria station. Originally it was planned that the Empire flying boats should operate from a base at Langstone Harbour, near Portsmouth, which would be served by through portions detached from Victoria-Portsmouth trains at Farlington. Later it was decided to operate from Southampton Water but still to run the 'Imperial Airways Specials' from Victoria. In the absence of a direct connection between the Central and Western Sections at Clapham Junction the trains joined the Western Section at Wimbledon, reached via Balham and the Streatham junctions. In the up direction the route from Wimbledon was via East Putney, Longhedge Junction and Stewarts Lane. The service was short-lived. Beginning in 1939, it was soon overtaken by the advent of World War 2. In recent years the Streatham-Wimbledon line has been used by coal trains to the depots at Tolworth and Chessington coming from the West London line.

The continuing growth of suburbs served by the Western Section was the reason for a new branch 4½ miles long from Motspur Park on the Epsom line to Chessington, opened throughout on 28 May 1939. It was still the age of local freight by rail and sizeable goods yards were provided at Tolworth and Chessington South. Both have served since as coal concentration depots. The Wimbledon-Sutton line had a yard at St Helier to serve a LCC estate of some 10,000 houses. A proposed extension of the Chessington line to Leatherhead which could have formed a Chessington loop matching the Hounslow loop on the Windsor lines did not materialise.

A landmark at Wimbledon on the main line into Waterloo was created in 1936 by the opening of a flyover which took the up local line over the fast lines and brought it alongside the down local. The rearrangement of tracks avoided conflicting movements at the approach to the terminus and was part of the resignalling with colour lights from Waterloo to Hampton Court Junction. An approach ramp at 1 in 60 brings up local trains on to a nine-span bridge of steel and concrete construction, followed by a descent at 1 in 45 to the level of the down local line. The new all-electric

signalbox was brought into use on 18 October 1936, replacing the old 'A' box which had been in use for some 44 years. Between Waterloo and Hampton Court Junction 13 signalboxes took over the work of 23 in service previously.

In its angular concrete lines the new box at Waterloo matched the style the Southern Railway was adopting in rebuilding stations. Wimbledon had been a forerunner of this concrete phase in 1929 although as late as 1933 Exeter Queen Street was rebuilt as Exeter Central in a 'civic building' style which met with some criticism from functionalists on the grounds that it could be mistaken for a town hall or public library. The exteriors of the concrete stations of later years were more akin to the façades of the super cinemas of the period. The use of this material was a legacy of the South Western which had opened a concrete depot at Exmouth Junction in 1913 where precast concrete components for many purposes, including buildings and bridges, were produced.

Light railways and joint lines were not covered by the Railways Act of 1921 which created the four Groups. From 11 May 1898 the South Western had a narrow-gauge neighbour at Barnstaple — the 1ft 11½in gauge Lynton & Barnstaple Railway (L&B). The Southern was given powers to buy the line in 1923 and did so for £31,000. In 1925 the Southern added to the L&B's stock of four locomotives with the 2-6-2T *Lew*, built for the line by Manning Wardle. *Lew* carried the word 'Southern' on its side tanks from the first.

The Lynton & Barnstaple ran for 19½ miles through picturesque country to the top of the cliffs at Lynton. Its founder, the publisher Sir George Newnes, had earlier provided Lynton with a cable line to the foot of the cliffs at Lynmouth, and after the railway was opened he pioneered road feeder services by operating horse-drawn coaches between Ilfracombe and Blackmoor station of the L&B in order to improve communication between Ilfracombe and Lynton. In 1903 he replaced them with motor wagonettes but this venture was unpopular in an area where the horse was still supreme, and the police complained of speeding if the wagonettes exceeded 8mph.

Under the scrutiny of the Southern Railway the L&B was seen to be a loss-maker and in spite of public protests the line was closed at the end of the 1935 summer service. All ended sadly in an auction at the Pilton depot on 13 November 1935. The scene depressed a correspondent of The *Railway Magazine* who wrote: 'The lines outside the carriage and wagon sheds presented an extraordinary appearance with the whole of the rolling stock on view to prospective purchasers, who examined the various "lots" with a familiarity most annoying to those whose recollections of happy holidays were associated with the little railway'. The locomotives fetched between £35 and £52. They were sold minus their nameplates, which went to the Railway Museum at York (then still on its old ex-locomotive depot site). Carriages went for between £10 and £13 10s.

Up to 1923 the Somerset & Dorset Railway had been leased by the London & South Western and the Midland. As a joint line it did not come under the Railways Act and it was transferred to the Southern and the London Midland & Scottish Railways by separate Parliamentary powers obtained in 1923.

In one area the railway was slow to bear the Southern imprint. Three Isle of Wight railway companies came into the Southern Group. As their locomotives were withdrawn they were replaced by old Brighton and South Western engines. As late as the mid-1920s a train of non-corridor coaches headed by an Adams '02'

Above:
**The Lynton & Barnstaple Railway opened in May 1898, and was acquired under an agreement by the LSWR In 1922. In this view one of the five engines, a 2-6-2T No 761 *Taw* leaves Barnstaple for Lynton in the winter of 1934.** Real Photographs (FEB 84)

Left:
**Lynton station was perched high above the town. The line suffered from road competition and was closed on 29 September 1935. The crew pose by their engine, No 759 *Yeo*.** Real Photographs

Below:
**Waiting to run round its train, 'M7' 0-4-4T No 481 stands at the end of the Lymington branch in June 1928.** H. C. Casserley

class 0-4-4 tank on the Ryde to Ventnor line looked pure South Western. Sixteen tank engines of that class worked on the Island. In other respects, probably of more interest to the average traveller, train services reflected the unity brought about by Grouping. A named train, the 'Tourist' appeared in the 1930s, running between Sandown and Freshwater via Newport over the lines of the former Isle of Wight and Freshwater, Yarmouth & Newport companies. Other services labelled 'East and West Through Train' followed the same route or ran between Ryde and Freshwater. The Island's holiday traffic was an important source of revenue to the South Western and Brighton companies as soon as they reached Portsmouth. In 1880 they had joined forces in building a pier and a railway line from the pierhead to join the Island's railway system at St John's Road. Previously passengers had been taken by a horse tramway between the ferries and the railway station.

The years 1935-36 saw the resignalling of 13.5 miles of main line between Waterloo and Hampton Court Junction, involving the replacement of the old semaphore signals with colour lights. At this time an average of 1,500 trains were dealt with at Waterloo each weekday, and in anticipation of a further increase in traffic resulting from the extensive electrification programme, work began on two important engineering projects. The first was to build a new flyover junction to the east of Wimbledon station, so that better routeing of trains could be obtained in this heavily congested area. The second was the Waterloo area resignalling, which involved extensive track remodelling at the terminus itself. This took place during the night of 16-17 May 1936, when 1,000 men calmly proceeded to carry out the great 'changeover'. To quote the words of the late Mr E. P. Leigh Bennett: 'At midnight Waterloo station was placed under a sort of anaesthetic while a major (and dangerous) operation was performed on its vitals, many of which were cut out and put back in a different place'. The whole operation took just 7hr. Resignalling with colour lights between Waterloo and Malden (except at Waterloo station) took place on 17 May 1936; Malden to Hampton Court Junction came into use on 28 June.

At Waterloo station the old semaphore signalling was replaced on 18 October, at which time six signalboxes between Waterloo and Vauxhall were scrapped and replaced with one new all-electric box, just outside Waterloo station, which today is a familiar landmark to the travelling public. In total, 13 boxes were taken out of use between Waterloo and Hampton Court Junction, the Southern Railway finding it necessary to build only two new ones, at Surbiton and Hampton Court Junction. Existing boxes at other selected locations were modernised and extended where additional space was required to house the new equipment. Bringing the new box

Far left Top:
**Before 1936, six signalboxes were required to control the movement of trains between Waterloo and Vauxhall; in this view the old 'A' signalbox stands over the complex track layout at Waterloo.** W. Waylett Collection

Far left Bottom:
**A signalman's view from the old 'A' signalbox, looking towards Vauxhall. Many of the gantries carrying the old semaphore signals were converted to carry colour lights.** W. Waylett Collection

Above left and left:
**Interior views of the old mechanical 'A' signalbox and the spacious new all-electric box with its large Westinghouse power frames.** W. Waylett Collection

into use took planning of almost military precision. After the arrival of the 11.58pm from Dorking due at 12.47am and the 11.48 from Windsor due at 12.41am, the existing Waterloo 'A', 'B' and 'C' boxes closed down. All lines at Waterloo and between Waterloo and Loco Junction had to be in the possession of the Signal Engineer by 1am sharp. The signalling staff at 'A' box, having closed down at 1am, had to proceed to the new signalbox ready to commence operation from 1.30am. Between then and 7am only the down and up main lines between Waterloo and Loco Junction, together with Platforms 1, 2, 3 and 4 were available for use. The first train to take its orders from the new colour lights was the 1.30am newspaper train to Yeovil.

Right:
**Signalboxes in service shown on left**
**Signalboxes abolished shown on right**
**Numbers above boxes indicates number of levers**

Below:
**Today's familiar landmark, the 'new' Waterloo signalbox brought into use in 1936 replacing six old mechanical boxes — Waterloo 'A', 'B' and 'C' and Vauxhall East, West and 'D'. The relay room, power switchboard, main power step-down transformers, rectifiers, battery room, and linesmen's quarters all occupy the lower part of the building.** Ian Allan Library

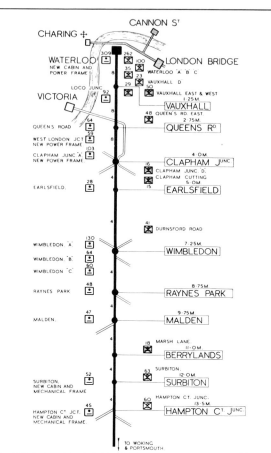

# Marine Matters

Under the Southampton Docks Company the port had been progressively improved to meet growing traffic. When the addition of the Empress Dock in 1890 proved insufficient to meet still-growing demands, the company was running out of finance and the London & South Western Railway was empowered to purchase the docks so that growth could continue. Of the further improvements undertaken by the LSWR, the one most apparent to travellers was the opening of the Ocean Dock in 1911 to accommodate the largest liners of the White Star company. Cunard came to Southampton in 1920.

The later 1920s saw the launch by the Southern Railway of the Docks Extension Scheme which converted some two miles of barren land to the west of the original docks into deepwater quays, adding greatly to the capacity of the port. A large area of land behind the quays was reclaimed in the course of the work and made available for industrial use. It went without saying in those days that both the shipping and the industrial facilities were rail-connected. A graving dock big enough to take a ship of 100,000 tons was opened at the eastern end of the extension of 26 July 1933. When the *Queen Mary* was in the dock for the first time the Southern ran excursions from Waterloo for the public to view the ship from the dockside.

On what were now Southern Railway shipping services from Southampton larger ships were put on the St Malo route in 1924. The *Dinard* and the *St Briao* were of 2,291 gross tons and could carry 1,340 passengers, with sleeping accommodation for 354. Three new ships were put on the Channel Islands service in 1930-31 — the *Isle of Jersey*, *Isle of Guernsey*, and *Isle of Sark*. Holidays with pay were bringing more Third Class traffic to the ships and these additions to the Channel Islands fleet made extra provision for it.

As has been noted earlier, the ships on the Portsmouth-Ryde service had been jointly owned by the LSWR and LBSCR since 1880. After taking them over on Grouping, the Southern Railway replaced five of them with new vessels between 1928 and 1935. In 1927 a new ship, the *Freshwater*, was put on the Lymington-Yarmouth route, and in the same year the company started a car ferry service between Portsmouth and Wootton in Fishbourne Creek. This early roll-on/roll-off venture was operated by the *Fishbourne*, a ferry with room for 16 to 20 cars in two rows and a passenger saloon. Cars drove on and off over a hinged ramp at each end. In 1928 the *Wootton* joined the *Fishbourne* and in 1930 a third ferry, the *Hilsea*, went into service.

# LONDON AND SOUTH WESTERN RAILWAY.

# SOUTHAMPTON DOCKS.

ONE hour and forty minutes from London (Waterloo). Position and facilities unrivalled.
Double tides. High water four times every day.
Never less than 28 feet at low water. Channel from the sea to the Docks dredged to 32 feet at LOWEST water. As safe by night as by day, being lighted by Gas Buoys.
Large Ocean Liners dock any hour, day or night.
"Prince of Wales" Dry Dock. 750 feet long, by 87½ feet wide at sill, and 112 feet at cope level. Depth to blocks 32½ feet H.W.O.S.T.
The New "Trafalgar" Graving Dock, 807 feet long, by 100 feet wide at entrance, and width at cope 125 feet, is now completed. This is the deepest Graving Dock in the United Kingdom, the depth to blocks being 35 feet H.W.O.S.T.
Passenger and Mail Trains go alongside Steamers. No Tender required.
Docks fully equipped with Hydraulic and Electric Appliances.
Warehouses Bonded and Free for the Storage of Wine, Tobacco, Provisions, Grain, &c.
Complete equipment of Grain Elevating and Conveying Machinery.
Spacious Sheds for Wood Goods under cover.
Specially constructed Coal Barge Docks, floating 14,000 tons of Coal in Lighters, ready for the Coaling of Line Steamers.
The finest installation of Cold Storage in the Kingdom is now complete.

L.S.W.

# SOUTHAMPTON *(continued)*.

The "South Western Railway" are owners of a fleet of large, fast, and comfortable steamers, performing the following services from Southampton :—

## To HAVRE for PARIS, SWITZERLAND, and SOUTH OF FRANCE

*DAILY (Sundays excepted)*.

The service being performed by New Geared Turbine Steamers, the feature of which are the special "Cabines-de-Luxe," with comfortable bedsteads.

SOUTHAMPTON - HAVRE offers unequalled advantages for Motorists, and the route enjoys the patronage of the Royal Automobile Club.

The powerful hydraulic cranes at Southampton Docks enable shipment of the car to be made at any state of the tide without the slightest risk. Special platforms obtained for the purpose.

Driving Licence obtained and all formalities for French Touring immediately on landing at Havre. Cars and Passengers travel by same steamer.

## To CHERBOURG for CENTRAL NORMANDY
*(Three times weekly)*.

## To ST. MALO for BRITTANY
*(Three times weekly)*.

Service augmented during Summer months.
The most direct route for BRITTANY, DINARD, DINAN, MT. ST. MICHEL, &c.

## To the CHANNEL ISLANDS

*DAILY (Sundays excepted)*,

from 1st June to 30th September, and three times weekly during the Winter months. (The service on the other three days is performed by the "*Great Western Railway*" steamers via Weymouth.)

The Company's "Guide to the Bathing Stations of Normandy and Brittany" will be sent free on application.

COMMUNICATIONS respecting Railway Passenger Traffic to be addressed to Mr. Henry Holmes, Superintendent of the Line, Waterloo Station, London; and Railway Goods Traffic to Mr. J. Smeal, Goods Manager, Waterloo Station, London; all communications on Dock and Steam Packet Business to be addressed to Mr. T. M. Williams, Docks and Marine Manager, Southampton.

H. A. WALKER, GENERAL MANAGER,
Waterloo Station, London.

B

In 1892 the LSWR acquired the entire estate of the Southampton Docks Company — one of the greatest master strokes in its history. No time was lost in transforming the port; dredging began at once and within a year the Inman Line had transferred its transatlantic steamers from Liverpool, and changed its name to the American Line. By 1897 the Royal Mail and Union Castle Lines among others were operating out of the port. Within six months passenger receipts were up 25%, imports up 32% and exports up by 36%. Dredging was only the beginning of the changes. An extensive area known as the 'Mudlands' at the mouth of the River Test was reclaimed and new quays were provided as well as an ocean dock. In 1895 the Prince of Wales Dry Dock was opened, measuring 750ft long and 87ft wide with an entrance of 112ft. Ten years later the Trafalgar Dry Dock was opened. At 875ft long, 90ft wide and with a 125ft entrance, it was able to accommodate the largest vessels afloat at the time. Cunard and White Star liners were attracted away from Liverpool, as Southampton-based ships could easily tap European markets by crossing the Channel to make calls at Cherbourg.

During the Southern Railway era even bigger and more expensive projects were undertaken, under the guiding hand of Sir Herbert Walker. The year 1924 saw the arrival from Tyneside of the world's largest floating dock — 960ft long and 130ft wide. Next came the most ambitious plan of all — the reclamation of a further 400 acres of the 'Mudlands' in order to provide a new 1½-mile long Ocean Quay. In 1927, work began on a new

Above:
**Progress is well under way on the reclamation of the 400-acre site of the new Western Docks in the Test Estuary, seen here in 1933. The South Western Hotel can be seen in the right foreground.** Ian Allan Library

graving dock, which again was the world's largest, taking six years to complete. At its peak, ships from some 30 companies were using the docks, with all the world's largest and fastest liners regularly seen there. During World War 2, Southampton was heavily bombed, and for a time all ocean traffic was suspended. After the war, recovery took time in view of the damage sustained. Since then the most notable development was the building of a new Ocean Terminal erected by British Railways to replace the buildings destroyed during the war around the Ocean Dock.

Left:
**The new Ocean Terminal, officially opened on 31 July 1950, was 1,270ft long and 120ft wide and housed a railway platform on the ground floor which was long enough to accommodate two complete boat trains. However, in 1983 the terminal had outlived its purpose and was demolished to make way for more useful devolopment.** Ian Allan Library

Above:
**An aerial view of the docks in 1950, the main areas are: 1 The Terminus station; 2 The Central station; 3 Rank Bovis McDougall Solent Mills; 4 King George V Dry Dock; 5 The Royal Pier; 6 The Town Quay; 7 Trafalgar Dry Dock; 8 Ocean Dock; 9 The Ocean Terminal; 10 Empress Dock; 11 The Inner Dock and 12 The Outer Dock. In this view there is no less than 495,888 gross tons of shipping at berth, including the world's three largest liners, the _Queen Elizabeth_, the _Queen Mary_ and the _United States_.** Ian Allan Library

Until June 1947 the only Pullman cars seen in regular service in Devon were those run by the GWR on the short-lived 'Torquay Pullman' in 1929. They had never been seen on Southern metals west of Basingstoke, until the introduction of the all-Pullman 'Devon Belle'. Its main objective was to serve Ilfracombe, although a Plymouth section was included. The train consisted at first of six coaches for Ilfracombe and four for Plymouth; in the summer months patronage sometimes demanded 14 coaches. A feature of this train was the special Observation Car attached to the rear of the Ilfracombe section of the train. The Devon Belle was booked to run non-stop to Sidmouth Junction, but such a journey of 159.75 miles was quite impossible as water capacity in the locomotive tenders was inadequate. To avoid a stop at Salisbury a change of engine took place at Wilton, making this the only train to run regularly through Salisbury non-stop. The 'Devon Belle' was booked to depart from Waterloo at 12 noon and made the 86.3-mile journey to Wilton in 107min, where 6min were allowed for a change of engine. Sidmouth Junction was reached 83min later, and after another stop of 4min the 'Devon Belle' was due in at Exeter Central at 3.20pm. Here the train was divided into two sections; the first, for Plymouth, left the Central station at 3.41pm with stops at Exeter St Davids, Okehampton and Devonport. Its arrival at Plymouth North Road was timed at 5.25pm, and at the Friary terminus at 5.36pm. The Ilfracombe section left Exeter Central at 3.48pm — again calling at Exeter St Davids, Barnstaple Junction, Barnstaple Town, Braunton and Mortehoe and terminating at Ilfracombe at 5.33pm, just over 5½hr from Waterloo. The up train had a slightly better timing of 5hr 20min. The Plymouth section left Friary station at 11.30am, half an hour before the Ilfracombe section.

At first the 'Devon Belle' only operated at weekends, but this was amended to five days a week from the summer of 1949. The summer of 1950 saw the withdrawal of the Plymouth section, which from then on terminated at Exeter Central and was then attached to the passing return up train. In 1952, owing to the lack of patronage, it was decided to confine the running of the 'Devon Belle' to Saturdays only, but it was later reinstated to run on Fridays, Saturdays and Sundays in the down direction. In the up direction it ran on Saturdays, Sundays and Mondays during the summer season only. The 'Devon Belle' was finally withdrawn at the end of the summer timetable in 1954.

Left:
**In its first year of service the 'Devon Belle' is seen speeding through West Weybridge behind 'Merchant Navy' Pacific No 21C15 _Rotterdam Lloyd_. The winged nameboards on the smoke deflectors of the locomotive were a unique feature of the train.** LPC/Ian Allan Library (23249)

Above:
**The new 'Merchant Navy' Pacifics were ideally suited for the 'Devon Belle', when fully loaded with 14 Pullman Cars. With passengers and luggage the train could weigh as much as 575 tons. Here, 'Merchant Navy' 4-6-2 No 21C4 *Cunard White Star* is seen nearing Milborne Port in 1947.**
L&GRP (9768)

Below:
**The Observation Car was not unique to the 'Devon Belle', but it was the first and only one to run on Southern metals. Complicated turning and remarshalling operations were necessary at both the London and Ilfracombe ends of the journey, to ensure that the Observation Car and Ilfracombe section were always at the rear of the train.**
Ian Allan Library

Fordingbridge

# The Years of Transition

The optimists who looked forward to nationalisation of the railways on 1 January 1948 as a new dawn, often ignored the effects of World War 2 and their influence on the future. In the war years the whole system had been stretched to the utmost. The railways had operated under a level of enemy attack never experienced before in this country while pushing their equipment to the limit. Recovery in the years ahead would inevitably be gradual.

In June 1945 the Western Section of what was still the Southern Railway had received the first of Bulleid's Light Pacific locomotives, the 'West Country' class, built on the same lines as the 'Merchant Navys' of the early war years but weighing 8¾ tons less. Neither class was easy to maintain and when the newly formed British Railways announced its requirements in the design of future standard steam locomotives it was clear that Bulleid's Pacifics did not conform.

Under British Railways all the 'Merchant Navys' were rebuilt, beginning in 1956, and a year later the first rebuilt 'West Country' appeared. The 'air-smoothed' casing was removed from both classes and three sets of Walschaerts valve gear replaced the former chain drive. Some 'West Countrys', however, were left in their original form which was 4 tons lighter than the rebuilds and so allowed a wider range of action west of Exeter, where the rebuilt engines were confined to the Plymouth road.

'Merchant Navys' and 'West Countrys' remained in service to the end of BR steam on the Southern and were responsible for many lively performances on the lines of the former London & South Western Railway, fully maintaining the traditions of the pre-Grouping and Grouping years. Some 'West Countrys' were given names associated with the Battle of Britain but were similar mechanically to the rest of the class.

Nationalisation brought the first of many changes of organisation. The former Southern Railway became the Southern Region and from 2 April 1950 all its lines west of Exeter were transferred to the Western Region although Waterloo still managed the trains and traction. Elsewhere the Region gained territory and it now took over the Weymouth-Channel Islands shipping services. There have been many changes of organisation and Regional boundaries since then but the signs were already ominous for the future of Waterloo as the terminus for trains to the far West Country.

As early as 1946 the Southern Railway had announced a pilot scheme for main line diesel-electric traction and Bulleid designed a one-off 500hp diesel-mechanical 0-6-0 shunter, but this did not appear until after nationalisation. The main line locomotives, also, were built after nationalisation, the first of them not being completed until 1951. All three were of 1Co-Co1 wheel arrangement, the bogies having the characteristic Bulleid segmental pivoting arrangement of his Co-Co 'booster' electrics but with an additional carrying axle within the frames. Nos 10201/2 were powered by an English Electric 16SVT engine similar to that in Nos 10000/01 on the London Midland but set to give 1,750hp at 750rpm. Some modifications were made in No 10203 which came out in 1954 and had a Mk 2 version of the 16SVT giving 2,000hp at

Right:
**Main line electrification reached Portsmouth in July 1937, via Woking and Haslemere. In June 1960, 4-COR EMU No 3153 heads a Waterloo-Portsmouth Harbour fast train through Vauxhall.**
J. Scrace

Below:
**A Waterloo-Portsmouth & Southsea stopping train formed by three 2-HAL units draws into Petersfield, past the site of the former Midhurst branch platform, in the mid 1960s.** John H. Bird

850rpm. At the same time the previous eight-step speed control was changed to continuous pneumatic control, giving the Southern Region a technical 'first' on British Railways. Continuous control has since become standard, improvements in engine design having put critical crankshaft speeds well outside the operating range. An early regular assignment of all three main line diesels was the 'Bournemouth Belle' Pullman. The first two had earlier worked to Bournemouth, Weymouth and Exeter but their availability was variable. All three went to the London Midland in the course of 1955.

A more permanent venture in diesel traction began in 1957 when two-car diesel-electric sets took over the services on a number of former South Western cross-country routes in Hampshire. Originally the sets had 500hp diesel engines but they were so successful in attracting traffic to the railway that a trailer had to be added in each set and the engine power increased to 600hp. The routes first served were from Portsmouth and Southampton to Winchester, Alton and Andover Junction. In a second phase of the scheme the services were extended over the Basingstoke-Reading line.

Another Southern Railway project that matured in British Railways days was a new Ocean Terminal at Southampton, opened on 31 July 1950. It was like a small modern airport on a reduced scale with VIP lounge, TV studio for interviewing arriving and departing celebrities and an observation area on the roof. There was a boat train platform inside the terminal. Soon after the opening, however, operation and management of the terminal and of other port facilities at Southampton were transferred to the Docks & Inland Waterways Executive.

Right:
**A single 2-HAL unit No 2665 passes through the Berkshire countryside near Ascot on an outer suburban Reading-Waterloo service in April 1968.** J. Scrace

Above:
**In 1875 the LSWR and Midland Railways jointly took over the lease of the 71.5-mile Somerset & Dorset Joint Railway, running from Bath to Bournemouth via Templecombe. The most famous train to run over the line was the 'Pines Express'. Introduced in 1910, it ran between Manchester, Liverpool and Bournemouth, via Birmingham and Bath. In the winter of 1962 all through passenger traffic was diverted away from the line, and total closure followed in March 1966. Here the 'Pines Express', with Southern Region 'West Country' class Pacific No 34043** *Combe Martin* **in charge of the Midland Region coaches, nears Templecombe in August 1962. Following its diversion away from the S&D to run via Reading and Basingstoke from the autumn of 1962, the 'Pines Express' was finally withdrawn from March 1967.**
Real Photographs (K5277)

During the war Bulleid had added to the stock of Southern Railway EMUs with 10 four-car sets which retained the contemporary Southern Electric look with a downward slope of the roofs over the driving cabs. They were criticised for their cramped Third Class compartments. In his next venture he was more generous with space, omitting one compartment per vehicle to give the others more room. These were the sets classified as 4-SUB. Roofs were level throughout but the cab fronts were slightly bowed. The 4-EPBs followed, the letters standing for 'electropneumatic brakes'. This type of braking, essential for quick deceleration on suburban services with frequent stops, was also fitted to the 4-SUBS but their designation was unchanged.

Like most suburban electrics except the stately Oerlikon stock on the London Midland, the Southern's EMUs were a humdrum lot to look at, and although the 4-SUBs and 4-EPBs at length kindled a surprising degree of affection on their home ground they created little interest elsewhere. It was quite different with the two-car restaurant/buffet sets Bulleid and his team designed in the early nationalisation period. One end of the kitchen vehicle was a buffet section styled in imitation of a Tudor pub with simulated oak panelling, settees and leaded windows. In the adjoining restaurant car the First Class section

carried on the same theme. Tables were arranged longitudinally, the diners sitting with their backs to the windows. In both classes the windows were shallow lights at head level, perhaps lest pleasant natural scenery without should divert attention from the ingeniously designed stage set within.

To cap the 'Olde Worlde' image, the buffets were called 'taverns' and observers were astonished to see this part of the exterior painted with artificial brickwork and half-timbering, with a

Below:

**The main line between Woking and Basingstoke was, and still is, famous for high speed runs. Here an unidentified 'King Arthur' 4-6-0 heads a down West of England express past an up Bournemouth express, hauled by rebuilt 'West Country' Pacific No 34029 *Lundy* in July 1959.** Derek Cross

Bottom:

**The RMS *Queen Mary* towers above Southampton Terminus as 'T9' 4-4-0 No 30732 starts a train for Southampton Central in May 1956.**
Ian Allan Library

Top right:
**A stopping train approaches Beaulieu Road in the New Forest behind 'T9' 4-4-0 No 30120 in November 1954.**
Ian Allan Library

Centre right:
**From the exceptionally long platform at Bournemouth Central it was possible to obtain a good view of the locomotive depot. In this 1957 view is 'Merchant Navy' Pacific No 35005 *Canadian Pacific*, 'Battle of Britain' Pacific No 34110 *66 Squadron* and two 'M7' 0-4-4Ts Nos 30111 and 30060 with a 'G6' 0-6-0 No 30260 in between.** R. A. Panting

Below:
**The Sidmouth branch was just one of many ex-LSWR branch lines to fall victim to the 'Beeching axe'. Here 'M7' 0-4-4T No 30670 is ready to depart with a train for Sidmouth Junction in June 1953.** Real Photographs (K1996)

simulated inn sign carrying an individual name for each car. At this time British Railways were experimenting with a standard carriage livery. It was the 'plum and spilt milk' livery era and Bulleid's scene-painting was in breach of the regulations. The first set went into service on the 'Atlantic Coast Express'. Others were drafted to the Eastern Region, but they were much ridiculed by Press and public, and were sent back to the Southern whence, as Eastleigh products, they had come. Soon orthodox seating and windows were put in the saloons and the quaint exterior decoration disappeared, but the buffets survived as built internally until remodelled on conventional lines in 1959-60.

Dr Richard Beeching became Chairman of the British Transport Commission in 1961, and when the British Railways Board was formed he was appointed its first Chairman in 1963. The results of studies of the railway situation carried out under his direction were published in two reports: 'Reshaping of British Railways' (1963) and 'Development of the Major Trunk Routes' (1965). They were crucial in their effect on the lines which had formed the old London & South Western Railway and shattered some dreams of former years. Exeter to Plymouth by the LSWR line was not seen as a major trunk route, and Waterloo-Exeter was viewed as a secondary service, mainly of importance in serving intermediate places along the way. Through services from Waterloo to stations beyond Exeter ended with the withdrawal of the 'Atlantic Coast Express' on 4 September 1964. Henceforth the Western Region operated the Waterloo-Exeter service throughout. Considerable stretches of line were singled and the trains stopped at most stations between Salisbury and Exeter. 'Warship' class B-B diesel-hydraulic locomotives provided the motive power.

Above:
**The climax of the heavily graded West of England main line was the 6-mile Honiton Bank leading to Honiton Tunnel. Here, 'West Country' Pacific No 34017 *Ilfracombe* pulls a West of England express up the 1 in 80 incline in the early days of British Railways in 1948.** L&GRP (15965)

Right:
**At Exeter St Davids it was possible to see trains from the Southern Region passing trains on the Western Region in opposite directions, bound for the same destination. In August 1962, 'West Country' Pacific No 34096 *Trevone* arrives with the through Brighton-Plymouth train.**
Real Photographs (K5285)

Right:
**'T9' 4-4-0 No 30709, at the head of an Exeter-Plymouth stopping train, stands in the spring sunshine at Okehampton in 1959. The line between Meldon (2 miles from Okehampton) and Bere Alston closed in May 1968. Passenger services on the Okehampton line were withdrawn in June 1972.** Real Photographs (K3973)

Below right:
**Halwill Junction was the largest single-line junction in the country. For a short while each day it became a hive of activity as trains from Exeter, Padstow, Bude and Torrington converged and spoiled the peace of this normally quiet location. In this view Standard Class No 41248 leaves for Torrington via the North Devon and Cornwall Junction Railway. Opened in 1925 by the Southern Railway, the ND&CJR was the last line to be constructed in the West Country.**
Real Photographs (K6633)

The former LSWR lines west of Exeter became known as the 'withered arm'. A service was maintained over the Plymouth Road between Exeter and Okehampton until 5 June 1972 but the continuation to Bere Alston, except for the few miles kept open to serve Meldon Quarries, had been closed on 6 May 1968. On the long meander from Meldon Junction to Padstow, trains were withdrawn from the Meldon Junction-Wadebridge section and from the Halwill Junction-Bude branch on 3 October 1966. The Halwill Junction-Torrington line had lost its train service on 1 March 1965. Exeter-Barnstaple remained open but trains stopped running to Ilfracombe on 5 October 1970.

All that remained at the Plymouth end of the old main line were the 11½ miles from Bere Alston to St Budeaux where trains joined the Western Region main line by means of a connection which had been put in during World War 2. They provided a 'basic railway' service between Plymouth and Gunnislake via Bere Alston, where reversal was necessary to join the short remnant of the Bere Alston-Callington branch. These lines were a legacy of that dependable South Western ally, the Plymouth, Devonport & South Western Junction Railway (PD&SWJ), but the section from Callington to the River Tamar at Calstock had begun life as the 3ft 6in gauge East Cornwall Mineral Railway, built to convey products from a mining area to the river for shipment. At Calstock there was a considerable difference in level between the railway and the river quays. A cable-worked incline lowered wagons to the quayside.

In 1908 the PD&SWJ acquired the East Cornwall line and converted it to standard gauge, equipping it at the same time for passenger traffic.

Left:
**Under the Beeching plan, the Southern suffered badly to the west of Salisbury, all branch lines to the coast being closed with the exception of the Exmouth branch from Exmouth Junction. At Budleigh Salterton, on the Tipton St Johns-Exmouth line, smoke still stains the brickwork of this road bridge in July 1984.**

Below left:
**The Avon Valley line from Alderbury Junction to West Moors closed in 1964. Here, Breamore station lies derelict in July 1983.**

Below:
**Of all the former LSWR lines affected by the Beeching proposals, those located in Devon and Cornwall suffered the most closures. Today the only passenger routes remaining are those from Plymouth to Gunnislake, Exeter to Barnstaple and the Exmouth branch. The old main line from Crediton to just west of Okehampton remains open for freight only, serving the stone quarry at Meldon. This view shows the track bed of the Barnstaple to Ilfracombe line, which closed in 1970.**

It also built a connecting line from Bere Alston to Calstock which crossed the Tamar on a viaduct of 12 arches of 60ft span and joined the old line at the top of the incline. Here the railway was 113ft above the quays and a steam-operated wagon-hoist with a capacity of one 10-ton wagon at a time was built to lift wagons up and down. Under the Southern Railway the hoist continued to be used, mainly for brick traffic, but when this declined the hoist was dismantled at the end of 1934. Gunnislake, the present terminus of the line, is the station beyond Calstock on the Cornish side of the Tamar. The quite impressive viaduct has survived and passengers today pass the site of the hoist, once one of the highest of its kind, as their train reaches the Cornish bank of the river.

When the 'Warship' locomotives were withdrawn the Waterloo-Exeter trains were worked by Class 33 diesel-electrics. This class was equipped

Unusual workings and special trains run in connection with impending line closures have always proved popular among railway enthusiasts. Passenger services were withdrawn in 1932 on the Bishop's Waltham branch, but freight survived until April 1962. Here an enthusiasts' special headed by 'M7' 0-4-4T No 30110 with push-pull set No 36 stands at Bishop's Waltham station in May 1953.
Real Photographs (K1791)

Right:
The end of steam on the Southern Region provided the opportunity for a variety of motive power to show its worth on many special runs. In this view former LNER Top Link Driver Bill Hoole watches 'A4' Pacific No 60024 *Kingfisher* as she speeds through Farnborough in March 1966 with an A4 Preservation Society special. R. B. Lifford

Below right:
The announcement of the closure of the freight-only line from Barnstaple to Meeth, brought about several 'Last Atlantic Coast Express' specials. The honour of being the last 'ACE' from Waterloo to Torrington went to this Ian Allan special in October 1982.

Charter control      2nd
Atlantic Coast Express
Saturday, 16th October, 1982
Waterloo
to
Barnstaple, Bideford and
Torrington and back
Organised by Ian Allan Ltd. to
Celebrate 40 years of Railway
Publishing
For conditions see over (S)    5844A

0102
0102

Left:
**The Andover Steam Event in March 1986 saw the running of this DMU special from Andover to Dinton station, which closed in March 1966, via the reinstated Laverstock loop.**

Below:
**The 'Blackmore Vale Express' marked the return to steam on the Southern with a series of special runs from Salisbury to Yeovil Junction in October 1986. The BVE returned again for a second season in June 1987, which also included a special run from Salisbury to Andover. Here 'Merchant Navy' Class No 35028 *Clan Line* prepares to return to Salisbury after being turned at Yeovil Junction.**

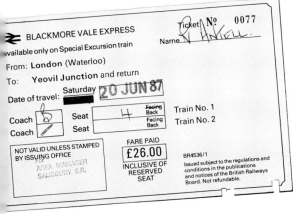

BLACKMORE VALE EXPRESS
Ticket No 0077
Available only on Special Excursion train
Name
From: **London (Waterloo)**
To: **Yeovil Junction** and return
Date of travel: Saturday **20 JUN 87**
Coach | Seat 4 | Facing Back | Train No. 1
Coach | Seat | Facing Back | Train No. 2
NOT VALID UNLESS STAMPED BY ISSUING OFFICE
AREA MANAGER SALISBURY S.R.
FARE PAID **£26.00** INCLUSIVE OF RESERVED SEAT
BR4536/1 Issued subject to the regulations and conditions in the publications and notices of the British Railways Board. Not refundable.

from the first for electric train heating. Loads were therefore limited to eight coaches because the diesel engine had to supply both heating and traction power. The Waterloo-Exeter service was improved in 1980 when Class 50 locomotives and Mk 2 coaches were allocated to the route. At the same time the Southern put on more Waterloo-Salisbury trains, working them push-pull with Class 33 locomotives. There were signs of traffic revival along the line when the former Sidmouth Junction station was reopened and named Feniton in 1971. More recently the Southern Region was encouraged by local demand to reopen Temple-combe in 1982.

Even before the first Beeching report the future of railways in the Isle of Wight had been in

**Right:**
**Barnstaple is now the railhead for the whole of North Devon. For the summer timetable of 1980 only, a through train between Barnstaple and Waterloo ran in the up direction on Saturdays only. In July 1980, Class 25 diesel No 25048 waits to depart from Barnstaple.**

**Below right:**
**Gunnislake is now the end of the line for the former PD&SWJ branch to Callington which is run as a basic railway, the survival of the line being largely due to the poor road access in the area. In this view a DMU painted in British Telecom yellow livery forms the return service to Plymouth.** Lens of Sutton

**Below:**
**Passenger services on the Eastleigh to Romsey line were suspended in January 1969. Here a 'Hampshire' DEMU departs from Chandlers Ford forming the 15.18 service to Eastleigh in 1968.** John H. Bird

question. Amid much local outrage the Newport-Freshwater line was closed in 1953 and Newport-Sandown in 1956. The 'reshaping' report of 1963 was clearly ominous for the Island railways and in 1964 there were proposals for complete closure of the system. There were protests to the Minister of Transport and in the end the Southern was required to maintain a service between Ryde and Shanklin. It was done as economically as possible by electrifying the line at 630V dc, simplifying layouts and signalling, and operating it with obsolete London Transport tube trains from the Central, Piccadilly and Northern Lines. They were reconditioned internally and modified electrically to return current through the running rails instead of through an insulated fourth rail. Today the stock is formed into five-car units (Class 485) or two-car (Class 486). Motorcoaches are each powered by two 240hp traction motors. When the trains were delivered to the Island they were already between 33 and 44 years old, but comparatively young and sprightly compared with the ex-LSWR Adams Class 02 0-4-Ts which they replaced, whose design dated back to 1889.

Top left:

**In 1979 new Class 508 EMUs were introduced to suburban lines operating out of Waterloo. Here No 508005 arrives at Virginia Water with a Staines-Weybridge train in April 1983. Most of this class have since been transferred to the London Midland Region for use on the MerseyRail services following the introduction of the Class 455 EMUs.**

Top right:

**The high-density 4-VEP EMUs were originally built for the Bournemouth line electrification in 1967 but they are now used on many outer suburban services from Waterloo. In this view two units arrive at Farncombe with a stopping train to Portsmouth in April 1983.**

Above:

**A 4-REP EMU leading two 4-TC trailer sets forms a Weymouth-Waterloo train as it speeds through the New Forest near Beaulieu Road in May 1977. During 1987 the 4-REPs were being withdrawn to release their traction equipment for use in the new Class 442 five-coach EMUs scheduled to be introduced on the newly electrified Weymouth line in 1988.** J. G. Glover

**Ride the North Devon Line**

Make the most of the N[...]
–Ride the North D[...]
Information, Train Ti[...]
Do and Places [...]
Until 11 May[...]

Have a goo[...]

**Starting 12 May 19[...]
NEW THROUGH
SERVICE BETWE[...]
STAINES & WOK[...]**

EGH[...]
VIRGINI[A]
WATER[...]
CHERTSEY
ADDLESTONE
BYFLEET
& NEW HAW
WEST
BYFLEET

Through journey Time[...]
Staines/
Woking
now less than
half an hour

We're getting there ≷

Now there is
a fast train
every hour
between
**Weymouth
Dorchester
Poole
Bournemo[uth]
Southamp[ton]
and Londo[n]**

404
91

see inside for service[s]
6 May 1974 to 4 May[...]

≷ Sou[thern]

See the beautifu[l]
Tamar Valley
by train

Centre
[So]uth

**Starting 12 May 1980**

**Faster,
and more
frequent
through
trains**

between
**WATERLOO
WOKING
BASINGSTOKE
SALISBURY
EXETER**

**12 May 1980 to
10 May 1981**

≷ Southern

0 **7067**
≷ BRITISH RAIL (S)
2nd - OFF PEAK
**CHERTSEY**
FARE 01.5[...]
(5553B)
to
**WOKING**
VALID
as dated
By
authorised trains[...]
AND BACK
For condition[s]
enquire ticket o[ffice]
NOT TRANSFER[ABLE]

0 **4526**
≷ BRITISH RAIL (S)
2nd - CHEAP DAY
**COSHAM**
FARE 01.0[...]
(5896B)
to
**EASTLEIGH**
via Botley
VALID as
advertised
AND BAC[K]
For conditions
enquire ticket office
NOT TRANSFERABLE

Right:
**Southern Region Class 33
diesel-electrics replaced the
unreliable Western Region
'Warship' diesel-hydraulics on
the Waterloo-Exeter line. Here
a Class 33 heads a down train
past Stowell, west of
Templecombe in July 1979.**

**Left:**
In May 1980, Western Region-allocated Class 50s replaced the Class 33s on the Waterloo-Exeter services, reducing the journey time by 25min, on the fastest timings. Here a Class 50 speeds through the now-closed Seaton Junction station, before the long climb up Honiton Bank in July 1984.

**Below:**
The new 100mph Class 442 'Wessex Electrics', the flagships of Network SouthEast were introduced from May 1988. The first of the class, unit No 2401 rounds the curve at Lymington Junction on a Brockenhurst-Bournemouth running-in train on 12 February 1988.
David C. Warwick

*the* **Wessex Electrics**

*are here!*

British Railways Board (S)
**MICHELDEVER**
PLATFORM TICKET
Available one hour on day of issue only.
Not valid in trains. Not transferable.
To be given up when leaving platform
For conditions see over

The LSWR being the owners of Southampton Docks had long catered for ocean traffic, but on 9 April 1904 entered a new phase by introducing a service of express boat trains between Waterloo and Plymouth Devonport to serve the vessels of the America Line. The service was shared with the GWR who carried the mails — the passengers travelling with the LSWR. However, the tender capacity of the engines and lack of water troughs on the line necessitated a stop at Templecombe, and in 1910 the Plymouth boat train services were withdrawn, leaving the GWR to carry both passengers and mails.

**Above left:**

**On one occasion in May 1954, several transatlantic liners were diverted to Millbay Docks due to a tugman's strike at Southampton, and for a short time Southern boat trains were once again seen in Plymouth. Here 'T9' 4-4-0s Nos 30710 and 30709 haul a Southern Region boat train away from Millbay on 20 May 1954.** Ian Allan Library

**Left:**

**After the LSWR took charge of the docks, the America Line company adopted Southampton as its new UK terminus for four of its ships in March 1883. Southampton was soon to become the principal centre for shipping. The first transatlantic liner to arrive was the *New York* which docked on 4 March 1883, thus starting the port's long association with international shipping. To encourage American passengers still further to use 'The shortest route between Port and Capital' the LSWR built a set of luxury coaches and christened them the 'American Eagle Express'. Here a down SR 'Ocean Liner Express', headed by 'Lord Nelson' 4-6-0 No 859 *Lord Hood* speeds through West Weybridge in 1947.**
LPC/Ian Allan Library (23227)

**Above:**

**During the 1950s there was still a healthy flow of boat trains meeting passenger liners and cruise ships at Southampton Docks. For example, in 1958 there were 80 down, and 52 up 'Ocean Liner Expresses', with only one day showing no such workings. On 5 July that year the arrival of seven ships generated no fewer than 12 trains to Waterloo. On 2 July 1952 the 'Cunarder' boat train was introduced between Waterloo and Southampton Ocean Terminal in connection with the RMS *Queen Mary* and *Queen Elizabeth*. The up 'Cunarder' is seen in 1956 as it passes through Clapham Junction behind 'Lord Nelson' 4-6-0 No 30860 *Lord Hawke*.** Brian Morrison

---

## "No Passport" Excursions
## LONDON (WATERLOO)
### TO
# HAVRE
(See "Important Notice" below)

### A DAY ON THE FRENCH COAST
### EVERY MONDAY,
### WEDNESDAY and FRIDAY NIGHT
### from 27th MAY to 27th SEPTEMBER inclusive

| Outwards | | | | | | |
|---|---|---|---|---|---|---|
| LONDON (Waterloo) | ... | ... | ... | ... | ...dep. | 9* 5 p.m. |
| SOUTHAMPTON DOCKS | ... | ... | ... | ... | {arr. | 10 49 " |
| HAVRE QUAY | ... | ... | ... | ... | {dep. | 11 15 " |
| | | | | | ...arr. | 6‡ 0 a.m. |
| **Return** (following night) | | | | | | |
| HAVRE QUAY | ... | ... | ... | ... | ...dep. | 11†30 p.m. |
| SOUTHAMPTON DOCKS | ... | ... | ... | ... | {arr. | 6 0 a.m. |
| LONDON (Waterloo) | ... | ... | ... | ... | {dep. | 7B 3 " |
| | | | | | ...arr. | 8§59 " |

B—Buffet Car, Southampton Docks to Waterloo.
*—Seats in this train should be reserved in advance (fee 2s. 0d. per seat).
†—Embarkation on the steamer commences at 8.30 p.m. (Passengers should be on board at least 15 minutes before the advertised departure time).
‡—Passengers may remain on the steamer until 7.30 a.m.
§—8.56 a.m. on Sundays until 8th September; 9.13 a.m. on Sundays from 15th September.

BERTHS ON STEAMER NOT GUARANTEED

SEA PASSAGE IN EACH DIRECTION BY BRITISH RAILWAYS'
CROSS-CHANNEL STEAMER *NORMANNIA* (3,543 tons)

REFRESHMENTS OBTAINABLE AT MODERATE PRICES ON BOARD

| | RETURN FARE (Liable to alteration) | 2nd Class s. d. |
|---|---|---|
| ADULT | ... ... ... ... | **95/6** |
| CHILD (3 and under 14 years) | ... | 51/- |

HAND BAGGAGE—Excursionists are only permitted to take with them small hand bags and other small articles intended for their own personal use.

IMPORTANT NOTICE.—British Subjects and citizens of the Irish Republic, travelling on these excursions, may obtain, free of charge, an "Identity Card" (in lieu of passport) available for use on one occasion only. Other nationals must carry valid passports.
Passengers wishing to travel with "Identity Cards" must effect their bookings **ON THE DAY PRIOR TO THE DATE OF TRAVEL** at the Continental Enquiry Office, Victoria Station, London, S.W.I (Office hours—8.0 a.m. to 4.0 p.m.: Tuesdays and Thursdays, 8.0 a.m. to 8.0 p.m.).
A passport photograph of each passenger(except children under 16 years of age) must be produced for affixing to the "Identity Card". Children under 16 years of age not holding passports, although not requiring a photograph, must still obtain an "Identity Card".
Where valid British or Irish Republican passports are held by intending passengers, these should be used in preference to "Identity Cards". Passengers travelling with passports may effect their bookings in advance at the Continental Enquiry Office, Victoria Station, London, S.W.I (Postal address:—Continental Enquiry Office, P.O. Box No. 29, London, S.W.I); British Railways Travel Centre, Lower Regent Street, London, S.W.I: or at principal Travel Agencies. Commonwealth citizens and foreign nationals should enquire, before commencing their journey, whether a French Visa is necessary. Foreigners of certain nationalities will require United Kingdom re-entry visas, to be obtained before departure from the United Kingdom.
CURRENCY.—On the outward journey, excursionists will be permitted to exchange into French francs, at the Bureau de Change, Southampton Docks, an amount not exceeding the exportable limit of £50 in sterling notes.
On the return journey, they will be permitted to re-exchange into sterling an amount in French francs not exceeding that purchased on the outward journey.

SC. 2037 A.30
31/2/63   **BRITISH RAILWAYS**   [SEE OTHER SIDE
W. A. SMITH (Leeds) LTD.

# The Bournemouth Line Electrification

After publication of the modernisation plan for British Railways in 1955 the Southern Region gave priority to extending electrification to the Kent Coast. The work was done at 750V dc, a report on the choice of system in 1956 having agreed that this system should be retained in the Southern Region because of the extent to which it had been established there. The report did say, however, that 'the ac system might be introduced in the western part of the Region if and when electrification of that area takes place'.

With electrification to the Kent Coast completed, the Bournemouth line was virtually the only remaining Southern Region main line not yet worked with electric traction. Authority to electrify as far as Bournemouth was given in 1964 but at that time the rest of the line to Weymouth was excluded. With 25kV ac electrification proceeding apace elsewhere this system had to be considered for Bournemouth. Three possibilities were studied: 25kV throughout from Waterloo; 25kV to Bournemouth from the end of the existing 750V dc system at Sturt Lane Junction (on the slow lines the third rail extended beyond Pirbright Junction to Sturt Lane and over the spur to Frimley Junction on the Ash Vale-Ascot line); or extension of the 750V dc system. The cost of the third option was found to be considerably less than that of the other two. The scheme included the 2¼ miles from Bournemouth to Branksome to give access to a maintenance depot and sidings to be built on the site of the former line to Bournemouth West, that station having been closed in 1965.

Once the work had begun the engineers were launched on a massive operation which included station rebuilding, track reballasting and welding, and resignalling as well as the electrification work itself. All this had to be done while the line was carrying a full steam service. It was an anomaly that Waterloo, the temple of Sir Herbert Walker's Southern Electric system, retained main line steam longer than any other London terminus.

Important technical developments had taken place since the Kent Coast electrification. The first substation with semiconductor rectifiers had been brought into use at Hollingbourne on the Maidstone-Ashford line in 1962. Oil-filled cables were able to withstand heating and cooling caused by changing loads without deteriorating. An improved system of fault detection had been developed that enabled substations to be more widely spaced by ensuring that a section in which a fault occurred would be isolated completely by the opening of the circuit-breakers at both ends. A multi-way control cable for rolling stock had been adopted to allow more switching functions to be performed and prepare for an operating policy described as 'the application of the multiple-unit principle to any formation of modern electric stock with electric or diesel-electric locomotives as might be required in the traffic pattern'.

In view of the need for diesel power over part of the route to Weymouth the conventional method of working would have been with locomotive-hauled stock and a change of traction at Bournemouth. However, space at Bournemouth was restricted and at Waterloo the platform lengths were inadequate for handling 12-coach trains and locomotives. On arrival of such a train there would be one locomotive at the buffers and another would have to be coupled at the 'country' end of the platform to take it out again. The combined train might then be fouling other tracks or preventing signals being cleared and points set for other movements at the terminus. In addition, paths for light engine movements would be difficult to find, and virtually non-existent in peak periods.

A novel operating system was adopted which involved propelling passenger stock at higher speeds than had been practised in this country before. A Waterloo-Bournemouth/Weymouth train was formed of a four-coach powered unit at the London end which propelled two four-coach trailer sets to Bournemouth. Here a Class 33 diesel-electric locomotive backed on to the front of the train, was coupled to the trailers, and proceeded to Weymouth with one or both sets. The powered unit crossed to the up line and waited for the arrival of coaches from Weymouth. These were propelled by a Class 33 which placed them straight on to the rear of the powered unit. The diesel then uncoupled and the complete train left for Waterloo with the powered unit leading. An interesting feature of the operation was that the diesel propelling the coaches from Weymouth was controlled by the driver in the leading driving trailer with a standard four-position EMU type controller.

Right:
**Approval for the electrification of the Bournemouth line was granted in 1964, the actual inauguration of electric services taking place on 10 July 1967. With less than a fortnight of steam working to go, rebuilt 'West Country' Pacific No 34024 *Tamar Valley* heads the 08.35 Waterloo-Weymouth out of Bournemouth on 29 June 1967.**
John H. Bird

Right:
**Under the provisions of the Bournemouth electrification scheme, fast services between Waterloo and Bournemouth would be provided by 12-coach trains consisting of a powered four-coach set (4-REP) at the London end and two unpowered four-coach driving trailer sets (4-TC) at the country end, one or both of the latter proceeding over the non-electrified section to Weymouth with locomotive haulage. On 7 March 1967, four months before the commencement of the full electric service, 4-REP unit No 3001 leads a typical formation into Basingstoke.**
D. E. Canning

The tractor unit of a Bournemouth train was a four-car set formed of an open standard class motorcoach at each end, a buffet car and a first composite. Each axle in the two motorcoaches was powered by a 400hp motor — the highest power used in Southern EMUs up to that time. In the Southern Region classification this unit was a 4-REP. It became BR Class 432 later. Although the route did not lend itself to very high continuous speeds it was commercially important to show a worthwhile gain in time over steam schedules. The 3,200hp of the tractor unit was necessary to achieve this and to observe the short turnrounds which had been planned to make maximum use of the rolling stock. Bournemouth/Weymouth trains were allowed 70min non-stop to Southampton and 1hr 40min to Bournemouth. In the last summer timetable (1987) before new EMUs were introduced the time to Bournemouth was 1hr 38min. The time to Southampton was still 1hr 10min but with a stop at Southampton Parkway (previously Southampton Airport).

The four-car trailer sets were classified 4-TC (later Class 438). At each end of the set there was an open standard class coach with driver's compartment. The other vehicles were a corridor first and a standard class brake vehicle with seating in compartments. All the 4-TC trailers and the trailers in the 4-REP sets were rebuilt from Mk 1 hauled stock. The motorcoaches, also, were basically Mk 1 vehicles. When introduced, all the Bournemouth line stock was painted in all-over blue livery.

The Bournemouth electrification was inaugurated on 10 July 1967. 'Farewell to Steam' specials had been run between Waterloo and Bournemouth on 2 July with 'Merchant Navys' Nos 35008 *Aberdeen Commonwealth* and 35028 *Clan Line*.

Many tales are told of surreptitious footplate rides in the last years of BR steam and Southern drivers seem to have been particularly obliging in this respect. Perhaps it is less well known that shortly before World War 2 the Southern Railway offered the public an opportunity to enjoy the experience officially. On 23 April 1939 an excursion was run from Waterloo to Brookwood, where passengers could queue for rides in the cabs of two Drummond 0-4-4 tank engines coupled back to back, which proceeded at a sedate pace up and down the Bisley branch (where a speed limit of 10mph prevailed). Two special tickets were issued, one for the journey to Brookwood and back, and the other for the 'Locomotive Excursion. As advertised. Available for trip on footplate from Brookwood to Bisley or vice versa'. Over 100 passengers were carried and towards the end of the day a 'cut price' ride was offered for those who wanted a second experience. Meals were available in dining cars parked at Brookwood and 'Lord Nelson' No 864 *Sir Martin Frobisher* was on view and open to all who wished to climb on board and handle the controls. In these days when footplate rides at steam centres are quite usual it is hard to realise what an innovation this excursion represented. Some lines in the United States were operating 'Rail Fan Excursions' at this period and

Above:
**The Weymouth portion of the 10.30 service from Waterloo, consisting of a 4-TC set powered by Class 33/1 diesel No D6536, is seen between Bournemouth and Branksome in the first month of non-steam operation — July 1967.** BR

passengers might be able to enjoy a novel view of the track from the rear platform of a baggage car or ride over freight-only lines, but the Southern's excursion was generally thought to be unique at that time. The fare, including the footplate ride, was 7s 6d.

The last public steam service out of Waterloo was a Southampton boat train which departed at 6.20pm on 8 July headed by 'West Country' Pacific No 34037 *Clovelly*. A lively account of events on that day was given by Klaus Marx in *Railway World* for July 1977. He joined a devoted band of watchers at Waterloo in the evening, one of whom had been there since 9am but had seen no steam, having just missed the departure of the 8.30am to Weymouth behind No 35023 with 'The End — The Last One' chalked on its smokebox door. Those who stayed on in the vicinity after the boat train had gone were rewarded for their patience and optimism. Watchers at Clapham Junction heard a Bulleid whistle and then saw the 5.30pm boat train from Weymouth guided through the station by 35023 again, still with the chalked inscription on the smokebox. The up 'Bournemouth Belle' was a disappointment. Steam had been promised but did not materialise. Class 47 No D1924 closed the 'Bournemouth Belle' chapter when it brought the Pullman into the terminus, for there was no 'Belle' on Sunday and with the new timetable on 10 July the Bournemouth line lost its longest-running Pullman.

In the new electric service 4-REP/4-TC formations worked the through Weymouth trains and those serving principal stations to Bournemouth. For stopping services four-car 4-VEP sets (Class 423) were provided. In these sets one intermediate vehicle was a motorcoach powered by four 250hp motors following the pattern set by the 'Brighton Replacement' stock of 1964 (Class 421/1). Similar units were later built in large numbers for general use in the Southern Region.

There was still considerable boat train traffic to Southampton in 1967, while the Channel Islands boat trains had been transferred from Paddington to Waterloo in 1959. These services needed locomotive power able to work schedules similar to those of the EMUs. Higher power was necessary than the 1,600hp of the Class 73/0 and 73/1 electro-diesels and the 1,550hp of the Class 33 diesel-electrics. It was provided by converting 10 2,500hp electric locomotives built for the Kent Coast electrification (Class 71) into electro-diesels. These formed Class 74 and had the advantage over straight electrics that they could operate on non-electrified dockside lines using their 650hp diesel engine. This was an advanced design with an electronic control system although it retained a form of the 'booster' principle first used in the Southern electric locomotives Nos 20001-3. Put into service with some haste for commercial

reasons, the class suffered from various problems, some quite minor and unforeseen such as the difficulty of keeping circuit boards and connectors securely plugged in despite the vibration inside an electric locomotive travelling at speed. There was also some optimism among the operators over what the 650hp diesel could achieve. One Class 74 turn started from Poole and was given the same timing over the non-electrified section to Branksome as a Class 33 of over twice the power. Late running at a peak business time did not please the local commuters.

The Class 74s shared with the earlier electro-diesels and Class 33 diesels compatability with

Top:
**The Class 33/1 diesels were not the only locomotives equipped to operate in the push-pull mode with 4-TC sets and some EMUs, this distinction being shared with, among others, the Class 73 electro-diesels. Class 73 No E6039 and a train of TC stock rest at Stewarts Lane MPD following a trial run in August 1967.** BR

Above:
**The stock for the 10.00 Bournemouth-Waterloo, formed by 4-REP unit No 3010 and two 4/TC sets, Nos 434/415, approaches Bournemouth from the direction of Branksome on 15 November 1976.**
Brian Morrison

EMU equipment. A Class 73/0 or 73/1 could replace a motorcoach in a Class 432 unit and advantage was often taken of this in the early days of the Bournemouth electrification when there was a shortage of EMU power. Boat train traffic to Southampton began to decline in the early 1970s until eventually there were only occasional workings in connection with cruises. The last Class 74s were withdrawn in 1977. Weymouth boat trains continued, often worked between Waterloo and Bournemouth by Class 73/1 electro-diesels, but from 1986 the timetable no longer showed a separate boat train service. Passengers for the Channel Islands travelled in a portion of a Waterloo-Weymouth train which was detached in Weymouth station and worked round to the quay.

By courtesy of the Southern Region, one of the writers had an opportunity to watch the handling of an EMU controller during a trip to Bournemouth in the cab of the leading driving trailer of a 4-REP/4TC formation. The first notch is for shunting purposes and there was no occasion to use it on this journey. Notch 2 (motors in series) started the train under automatic acceleration and was held until we coasted for the curve at Vauxhall. The driver then went into Notch 3 (motors in parallel) for further acceleration, returning momentarily to Notch 2 later to keep speed within the 65mph limit which was then in force until New Malden. It was raised to 70mph from Clapham Junction to New Malden in 1978. A driver cannot notch back direct, but to select a lower notch returns to 'off' and then advances the handle to the required position.

The full speed notch (Notch 4) was taken at Nine Elms, allowing the motors to go into weak field, but coasting through Clapham Junction and Wimbledon followed by Notch 3 until clear of New Malden ensured observation of the limit. After that there were long periods of running in Notch 4 interspersed with coasting for speed restrictions. Our first achievement of 90mph was at Byfleet, and after coasting through Woking a return to Notch 4 brought us back to 90mph by Pirbright, the speedometer hovering around this mark until power had to be cut before Hook to observe a speed restriction for permanent way work at Newham. Recovering speed in Notch 4 we had reached 80mph before coasting through Basingstoke. With power on again, we were up to 80mph at Worting Junction and still accelerating to reach 90mph at Roundwood Summit.

Once 'over the top' the speedometer stayed on the 90mph mark while coasting for most of the way through Micheldever and Winchester, only a short restoration of power in Notch 3 being needed to hold the speed. At Shawford we were still coasting at 90mph when a double-yellow signal aspect was sighted, changing to green as we approached.

Reduced speed was necessary in any case as we were approaching Eastleigh, passed in exactly the 62min allowed for the 73½ miles from Waterloo.

After passing Eastleigh, Notch 4 had brought us up to 68mph before power had to be cut to observe a temporary 20mph speed restriction. There was now no time for speed to rise much above 50mph in Notch 4 before we checked severely for the sharp curve at Northam Junction. During acceleration in Notch 4 the motors go into weak field at about 40mph. A slow finish through the Southampton suburbs brought us into the station in the scheduled 70min after leaving Waterloo.

Onwards to Bournemouth, 90mph was reached on two occasions, the first after New Milton station and again after recovering from a brief drop to 80mph. Then we coasted through Christchurch at 60mph and although the line speed was then 90mph the highest we reached before Bournemouth was 65mph. No doubt we should have done more 90mph running on the Southampton-Bournemouth stretch but for a double-yellow before Brockenhurst, followed by a yellow at the home signal warning us that the starter was 'on'. When we stopped in the station, Signal Engineer's staff who had been working on track circuits gave us leave to pass the next two signals at 'danger'. Pulling away cautiously in Notch 2 the driver soon moved into Notch 3 and we passed our second 'red' at about 40mph before resuming full-speed running. A lasting impression of this trip is of the absence of noise from the traction motors — no 'whine' during acceleration or constant hum at full speed. The reason, of course, was that the motors were eight coaches further back under the 4-REP unit that was propelling us and responding to the signals from the driver's controller transmitted over the multi-way control cable running through the train.

The ability of different types of motive power to work together was a key feature of operational planning for the Bournemouth electrification. It had enabled a diesel-hauled train and an EMU to be combined for part of a journey. An early example was the return working of a Waterloo-Salisbury train consisting of a Class 33 propelling a four-car trailer set. On the return journey, with the diesel leading, an EMU from Southampton was coupled in the rear at Basingstoke and the remainder of the run was made with the driver in the diesel controlling the locomotive and the motors of the EMU with the same power handle. Later the principle was extended to similar 'dual-power' trains from Waterloo with portions for Salisbury and Eastleigh which ran combined to Basingstoke and divided there, the diesel locomotive taking the leading four coaches to Salisbury while the EMU portion, usually two 4-VEP units, continued over the live rail to Eastleigh.

Above:
**The coaling plant is seen here in the final years of the Southern Railway.** Ian Allan Library

Nine Elms was the last main line steam shed to remain operational in the London area. Its closure in July 1967 marked the end of an era which had begun in 1838, when the Southampton Railway opened its Metropolitan Terminus. The first depot was built alongside the passenger and goods station and remained there until 1861 when continual expansion necessitated its resiting. The company decided to take the opportunity of purchasing some 30 acres of land on the south side of the main line for a new Locomotive, Carriage & Wagon Works and Engine Shed, so that the original site could be made available to the Goods Department. The first completed building was a 6-acre running shed designed to accommodate 100 locomotives. Four 40ft turntables and numerous coal stages were provided. Access to the main line was from Loco Junction situated just to the west of Nine Elms Junction. This awkward arrangement was dictated by the site and required the reversal of all engines using Waterloo.

Above right:
**An impressive line-up of locomotives, which includes examples of the 'Schools', 'King Arthur' and 'H15' classes, parades outside the running shed in August 1942.** Ian Allan Library

Right:
**Under British Railways, Nine Elms became depot 70A. It never acquired diesel servicing facilities and any diesel shunters working nearby were maintained at Norwood Junction, Feltham or Selhurst. It closed with the end of steam working on the Southern Region in July 1967. In this view taken just two months after closure, the old running shed stands empty, and a handful of locomotives await their removal to the scrap yard, as the weeds take control. Today the old Nine Elms site is covered by the new 'Covent Garden Fruit Market', served entirely by road. Any diesel locomotives working at Waterloo are now serviced at Stewarts Lane.** Graham S. Cocks

New developments in 1876 saw the provision of a new running shed, in the form of a semi-circular roundhouse with 26 running roads, off two adjacent 42ft turntables. When built, the roundhouse could take well over 100 engines. In 1855 the first stage of the construction of a new 15-road straight shed, with its own coaling facilities, had been opened. The second stage doubled the length from 180ft to 360ft and was carried out in 1889, all locomotive movements into and out of the shed being made via a 50ft turntable. The capacity of the depot was now well in excess of 200 engines. Due to the lack of space and the expanding goods traffic in the 1880s the Carriage & Wagon shops were transferred to Eastleigh, followed in 1909 by the Locomotive Works. Both these sites, along with the old semi-roundhouse, were taken over by the Goods Department to cope with the traffic between Southampton and Nine Elms. To compensate for the loss of the roundhouse a new 10-road shed was built adjoining the existing 15-road shed. This was completed in 1910, together with various staff amenities with a shed office alongside. After the completion of this 'new shed' there was very little further structural alteration to the depot. A modern ferro-concrete coaling and water softening plant was constructed in 1932. On the outbreak of World War 2, a turning triangle was installed as an insurance against damage to the turntable. The running shed continued to operate until the end of steam on the Southern in July 1967. Its principal duties were to provide locomotives for the services to and from Bournemouth and Salisbury and for local freight services out of Nine Elms.

SOUTHERN RAILWAY.
PULLMAN CAR TICKET.
Available for one journey on day of issue only,
when accompanied by Third Class Railway Ticket
(330)
(330)
From Waterloo
To Bournemouth Date
Depart 12·30 CHARGE 3/- Jan
0014
FOR CONDITIONS SEE BACK.

BRITISH RAILWAYS (S)
Pullman Car Ticket "Bournemouth Belle"
Bournemouth West to
SOUTHAMPTON CENTRAL
Pullman
Car Letter A Seat No.
Available for one journey on day of issue
only when accompanied by Third Class
Railway Ticket. Charge 1/9
FOR CONDITIONS SEE BACK.

3841    1941    3841

Left:

**Until its temporary withdrawal at the outbreak of World War 2, haulage of the 'Bournemouth Belle' was normally by a 'Lord Nelson' 4-6-0. Its reintroduction into service came on 7 October 1946, after which motive power was then normally supplied by one of the new 'Merchant Navy' Pacifics. Here No 21C11 *General Steam Navigation*, thunders through West Weybridge in 1947.** L&GRP (23248)

Bottom left:

**With a load of 12 Pullman cars, rebuilt 'Merchant Navy' No 35005 *Canadian Pacific* is seen near Southampton Central in May 1963.** R. A. Panting

Below:

**In April 1950 the up 'Bournemouth Belle' draws into Bournemouth Central, with 'Merchant Navy' No 35012 *United States Lines* in charge.**
D. Sutton Collection/Real Photographs (DS14)

Long before the introduction of corridor trains the LSWR used 'Pullman Drawing Room Cars', as they were officially called, on their principal express trains between Waterloo and Bournemouth. They were for the exclusive use of First Class passengers, who of course had to pay a supplement in addition to the normal fare. The introduction of restaurant cars brought about their demise and by 1921 all Pullman cars had been withdrawn. Pullman cars were not to be seen again on LSWR metals until 1931 and the introduction of the 'Bournemouth Belle'. It was originally to run on Sundays only, but from the beginning of 1936 it became a daily service with a 10.30am departure from Waterloo. It was booked to run the 79.2 miles non-stop to Southampton Central in 87min, arriving at 11.57am. Here, a 3min stop was allowed before running the 28.8 miles to Bournemouth Central, again non-stop, and arriving at 12.36pm. Another 3min stop was allowed before the short run to Bournemouth West where the train terminated at 12.47pm. In the up direction departure from Bournemouth West was at 4.35pm and from Bournemouth Central at 4.45pm — 33min being allowed for the run to Southampton Central (3min less than the down train). Arrival at Waterloo was at 6.46pm, making this the fastest train of the day from Southampton Central. Two were First Class cars, the others were Third Class vehicles and a Brake Third was provided at each end. In its final years the load often increased to 12 cars, sometimes with an additional bogie full brake, making this the heaviest train working on the Southern. Following the Bournemouth line electrification in the summer of 1967, the 'Bournemouth Belle' was withdrawn.

**By kind permission of Dalkeith Publishing Co**

# Postscript

The most enduring features of a railway are the work of the civil engineer. Over his embankments and through his cuttings and tunnels there passes an ever-changing panorama. Sometimes the rate of change is slow and different generations are merged in the overall picture. In recent years it has accelerated. The 4-REPs and 4-TCs (surely they will be remembered by their characteristically Southern labels) had worked the Bournemouth line for less than 20 years when the Region was authorised to extend electrification to Weymouth. The former push-pull operation would no longer be necessary and new five-coach express units were built, each with a motorcoach powered by a 1,600hp traction equipment salvaged from a 4-REP. Track improvements carried out in the 1985-86 period between Woking and Southampton allowed the maximum line speed to be raised from 90mph to 100mph and a reduction in overall journey times of 16 or 17min to be scheduled, the gain beyond Bournemouth being largely due to the better acceleration of the EMUs. The new stock is Class 442. Coaches are air-conditioned, with pushbutton-operated sliding doors, and conform to the body length of 23m (75.4ft) which is standard for vehicles based on the Mk 3 bodyshell. 'Cuisine 2000' catering is provided from a buffet. Driver training began in the December/January 1987-88 period and the new sets were introduced at a planned rate of one a week to meet the target of the 1988 timetable. Power was switched on between Bournemouth and Weymouth on 11 January 1988.

Withdrawal of 4-REP units to release their traction equipments left Bournemouth semi-fasts without a buffet car. Keeping pace with the withdrawals, 4-TC sets were reformed with a buffet car from a withdrawn 4-REP replacing one TSB (trailer standard brake). Sets treated in this way were classified 492/8. Power was provided by Class 73/1 electro-diesels working push-pull.

The sounds of a railway also change with time. On the South Western services out of Waterloo where Class 455 EMUs have replaced 4-SUBs and 4-EPBs the slamming of doors is no longer heard as a train discharges its load. The sound of steam has long gone, of course, but it survived surprisingly long in outer London on the Clapham Junction-Kensington Olympia shuttle.

Today Waterloo is a terminus in the conglomerate 'Network SouthEast'. Its renovation and repainting, and the many customer services in its wide, curving and uncluttered concourse have even earned praise in the Press — not always an admirer of things Southern. 'Network SouthEast' liveries or rolling stock tended to shock when first seen but 'custom reconciles us to everything' (the consoling words are Edmund Burke's). When Queen Mary opened the rebuilt Waterloo on 21 March 1922 by cutting a silken cord across the steps of the Victory Arch, the London & South Western was on the verge of becoming the Southern Railway. From Railway to Region and on to whatever lies ahead a long and distinguished tradition is a firm foundation to every change.

Right:
**Two Class 455 EMUs stand in the Windsor line platforms at Waterloo in October 1985. It is planned that this part of the station will be rebuilt to house the new Channel Tunnel terminus. To replace the platforms lost to the new terminal, extra platforms will be built between the existing Platforms 11 and 12, and 15 and 16, reducing the number of platforms available for the South Western services from 21 to 19.**

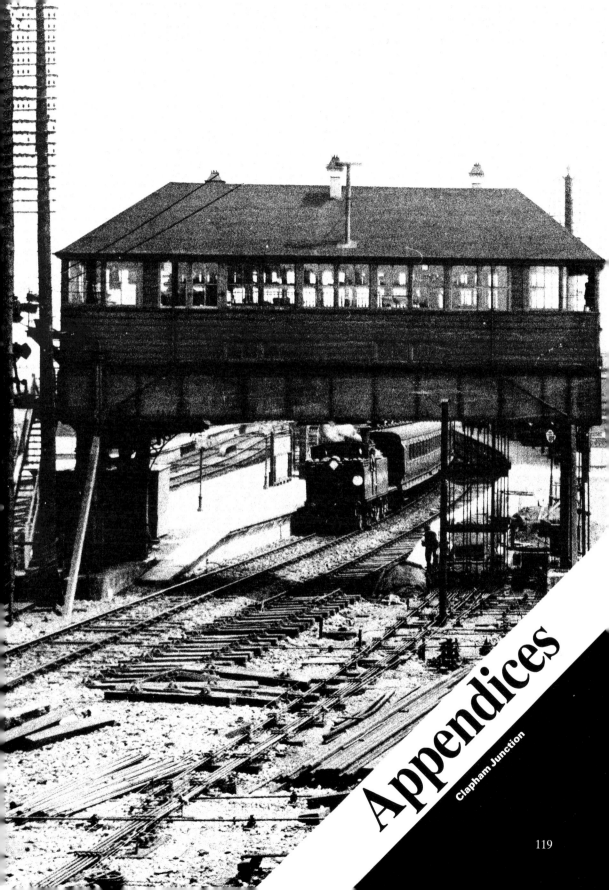

**Appendices**

Clapham Junction

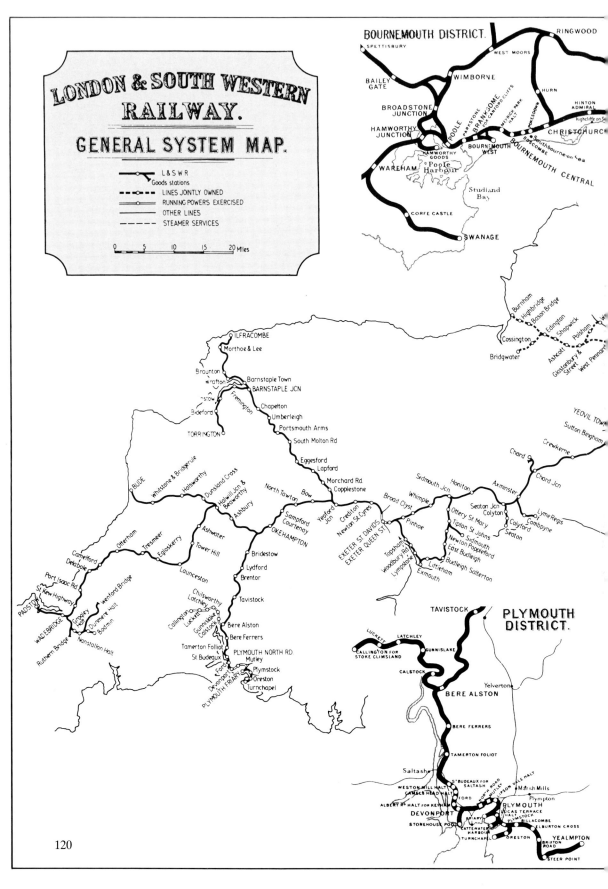

# LONDON & SOUTH WESTERN RAILWAY.

## GENERAL SYSTEM MAP.

L & S W R
Goods stations
LINES JOINTLY OWNED
RUNNING POWERS EXERCISED
OTHER LINES
STEAMER SERVICES

0   5   10   15   20 Miles

BOURNEMOUTH DISTRICT.

RINGWOOD
SPETTISBURY
WEST MOORS
BAILEY GATE
WIMBORNE
HURN
BROADSTONE JUNCTION
PARKSTONE
BRANKSOME
HINTON ADMIRAL
POOLE
MEYRICK PARK HALT
HAMWORTHY JUNCTION
POKESDOWN
BOURNEMOUTH WEST
Highcliffe on Sea
CHRISTCHURCH
HAMWORTHY GOODS
SOUTHBOURNE on Sea
BOSCOMBE
WAREHAM
Poole Harbour
BOURNEMOUTH CENTRAL
Studland Bay
CORFE CASTLE
SWANAGE

Burnham
Highbridge
Bason Bridge
Edington
Shapwick
Cossington
Ashcott Polsham
Bridgwater
Glastonbury & Street
West Pennard

YEOVIL TOWN
Sutton Bingham
ILFRACOMBE
Morthoe & Lee
Braunton
Crewkerne
Wrafton
Barnstaple Town
BARNSTAPLE JCN
Chard
Fremington
Chapelton
Chard Jcn
Bideford
Umberleigh
TORRINGTON
Portsmouth Arms
South Molton Rd
Eggesford
Lapford
Sidmouth Jcn
Honiton
Axminster
Lyme Regis
Morchard Rd.
BUDE
Whitstone & Bridgerule
North Tawton
Copplestone
Whimple
Seaton Jcn
Colyton
Combpyne
Holsworthy
Bow
Broad Clyst
Ottery St Mary
Colyford
Dunsland Cross
Yeoford Jcn
Crediton
Tipton St Johns
Seaton
Halwill Jcn & Beaworthy
Newton St Cyres
Pinhoe
Newton Poppleford
Sidmouth
Otterham
Ashbury
Sampford Courtenay
EXETER ST DAVIDS
Topsham
East Budleigh
Tresmeer
Ashwater
OKEHAMPTON
EXETER QUEEN ST
Woodbury Rd
Budleigh Salterton
Egloskerry
Tower Hill
Littleham
Camelford
Bridestow
Lympstone
Exmouth
Delabole
Lydford
Launceston
Brentor
Port Isaac Rd
St Kew Highway
Tavistock
TAVISTOCK
PLYMOUTH DISTRICT.
PADSTON
Chilsworthy
Latchley
Grogley Halt
Dunmere Halt
Callington
Luckett
LUCKETT
LATCHLEY
WADEBRIDGE
Wenford Bridge
Bodmin
Gunnislake
Bere Alston
CALLINGTON FOR STOKE CLIMSLAND
GUNNISLAKE
Ruthern Bridge
Nanstallon Halt
Bere Ferrers
CALSTOCK
Tamerton Folliot
Yelverton
St Budeaux
PLYMOUTH NORTH RD.
BERE ALSTON
Mutley
Ford
Plymstock
Devonport
Oreston
BERE FERRERS
PLYMOUTH FRIARY
Turnchapel
TAMERTON FOLIOT
Saltash
TIPSON VALE HALT
Marsh Mills
WESTON MILL HALT
St BUDEAUX FOR SALTASH
NORTH ROAD
Plympton
CAMELS HEAD HALT
Ford
Plymstock
ALBERT RD HALT FOR KEYHAM
PLYMBRIDGE HALT
Billacombe
PLYMOUTH
ELBURTON CROSS
DEVONPORT
FRIARY
LUCAS TERRACE HALT
STONEHOUSE POOL
CATTEWATER HARBOUR
TURNCHAPEL
Oreston
YEALMPTON
BRIXTON ROAD
STEER POINT

120

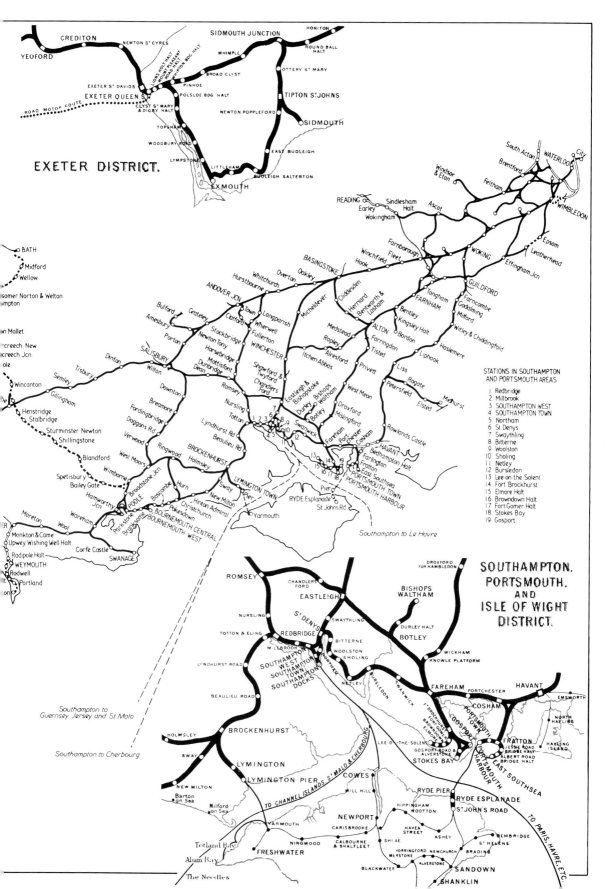

# Appendix 1  LSWR Locomotives 1872-1922

| Class | Wheel Arrangement | Duties | Total in class | Building dates | Builder(s) |
|---|---|---|---|---|---|
| **Beattie designs (father and son) 1850-1878** | | | | | |
| 273 | 0-6-0 (Double Frames) | Goods | 12 | 1872 | Beyer Peacock |
| 302 | 0-6-0 (Inside Frames) | Goods | 36 | 1874-78 | Beyer Peacock |
| 282 'Ilfracombe Goods' | 0-6-0 | Light Goods | 8 | 1873-80 | Beyer Peacock |
| 330 | 0-6-0ST | Shunter | 20 | 1876-82 | Beyer Peacock |
| 329 'Beattie Well Tank' | 2-4-0WT | Suburban Passenger | 85 | 1874-75 | Beyer Peacock |
| 348 | 4-4-0 | Express Passenger | 20 | 1876-77 | Sharp Stewart |
| 318 'Metropolitan Bogie' | 4-4-0T | Fast Passenger | 6 | 1875 | Beyer Peacock |
| **Adams designs 1878-95** | | | | | |
| 46 'Ironclad' | 4-4-0T | Suburban Passenger | 12 | 1879 | Beyer Peacock |
| 415 'Radial' | 4-4-2T | Passenger | 71 | 1882-85 | Stephenson Beyer Peacock Neilson Dübs |
| T1 F6 | 0-4-4T | Passenger | 50 | 1888-96 | LSWR (Nine Elms) |
| 02 | 0-4-4T | Passenger | 60 | 1889-95 | LSWR (Nine Elms) |
| 380 | 4-4-0 | Mixed Traffic | 12 | 1879 | Beyer Peacock |
| 135 | 4-4-0 | Express Passenger | 12 | 1880-81 | Beyer Peacock |
| 445 | 4-4-0 | Express Passenger | 12 | 1883 | R. Stephenson |
| 460 | 4-4-0 | Express Passenger | 21 | 1884-87 | Neilson R. Stephenson |
| 395 | 0-6-0 | Goods | 70 | 1881-86 | Neilson |
| A12 'Jubilees' 04 | 0-4-2 | Mixed Traffic | 90 | 1887-95 | LSWR (Nine Elms) Neilson |
| X2 T3 T6 X6 | 4-4-0 | Express Passenger | 60 | 1890 | LSWR |
| B4 K14 | 0-4-4T | Dock Shunter | 25 | 1891-93, 1908 | LSWR |
| G6 M9 | 0-6-0-T | Goods | 34 | 1894-1900 | LSWR |
| **Drummond designs 1895-1912** | | | | | |
| M7 X14 | 0-4-4T | Passenger | 105 | 1897-1911 | LSWR |
| 700 | 0-6-0 | Goods | 30 | 1897 | Dübs |
| T7 E10 | 4-2-2-0 (Non-coupled) | Express Passenger | 6 | 1897, 1901 | LSWR |
| C8 | 4-4-0 | Passenger | 10 | 1898 | LSWR |
| T9 | 4-4-0 | Express Passenger | 66 | 1899-1901 | LSWR, Dübs |
| K10 | 4-4-0 | Mixed Traffic | 40 | 1901-02 | LSWR |
| L11 | 4-4-0 | Mixed Traffic | 40 | 1903-07 | LSWR |
| S11 | 4-4-0 | Mixed Traffic | 10 | 1903 | LSWR |
| L12 | 4-4-0 | Express Passenger | 20 | 1904-05 | LSWR |
| F9 'Drummond Bug' | 4-2-4T | Inspection Car | 1 | 1899 | LSWR |
| F13 E14 E3 G14 P14 T14 'Paddlebox' | 4-6-0 | Express Passenger | 26 | 1905 | LSWR |
| D15 | 4-4-0 | Express Passenger | 10 | 1912-13 | Eastleigh |
| **Urie designs 1912-22** | | | | | |
| H15 | 4-6-0 | Mixed Traffic | 26 | 1913-25 | Eastleigh |
| N15 (later 'King Arthur') | 4-6-0 | Express Passenger | 20 (LSWR-built) | 1918-23 | |
| S15 | 4-6-0 | Mixed Traffic | 20 (LSWR-built) | 1920-21 | Eastleigh |
| G16 | 4-8-0T | Feltham Yard Hump Shunter | 4 | 1921 | Eastleigh |
| H16 | 4-6-2T | Goods | 5 | 1921-22 | Eastleigh |

# Appendix 2  The LSWR Preserved

Preservation plays a major role in keeping the spirit of the LSWR alive. Many working or static exhibits can be found in various collections, such as that of the National Railway Museum, which often lends out exhibits. Working locomotives and rolling stock can be seen on the Bluebell, or Isle of Wight Railways, while in the LSWR area itself there are two preserved lines — the Swanage Railway and the Mid-Hants Railway.

Take a nostalgic steam train ride in the beautiful Purbecks. Trains run most weekends from Easter to October and daily in peak holiday season.

Swanage station, Swanage Dorset
For more details ring (0929) 425800

Left:
**British Rail closed the branch to Swanage in January 1972. To mark the first stage of track relaying a new halt at Herston was opened at Easter 1984. Here, No 41708, on loan from the Midland Railway Trust at Butterley, has just arrived with a train from Swanage in August 1985.**  M. A. Stollery

Below:
**The Swanage Railway had been operating with a special licence from the Department of Transport Railways Inspectorate since 1979, but in June 1987 the railway was granted a Light Railway Order. This now means that the railway will be able to open as much of the line towards Wareham as possible. This snow scene shows the railway's terminus at Swanage in March 1986.**
Robin Brasher

**Top:**

The Mid-Hants opened the first section of their line between Alresford and Ropley in April 1977. In 1985 the line was extended to the BR station at Alton. The stations at Alresford, Medstead & Four Marks and Alton are all repainted in Southern livery, while at Ropley the clock has been turned back to the days of the LSWR. Ropley is also the location of the line's workshops, where locomotive and rolling stock restoration work is carried out. In this view, restored 'N' class 2-6-0 No 31874 arrives at Alresford with a train from Alton in September 1985.

**Above:**

On loan from the National Railway Museum, preserved 'T9' 4-4-0 No 30120 arrives at Medstead & Four Marks in September 1985, hauling one of the Mid-Hants Railway's Mk 1 coach sets.

**Right:**

Since 1970 it has been possible to travel along the track bed of the old Seaton branch as far as Colyton by taking a trip on one of the replica tramcars owned by the Seaton & District Electric Tramway. In this view one of the two-thirds scale tramcars heads along the banks of the River Axe towards Colyton in July 1984.

# Appendix 3  The Woking Homes

The LSWR Servants Orphanage was founded in 1885 by the Canon Allen Edwards, and with the help of local railwaymen, he rented a house in Jephreys Road, Clapham, and set up a home for orphaned children. From this small house in Clapham, a new 'home in the country' was opened by the Duchess of Albany on 5 July 1909, alongside the railway line at Woking in Surrey, with accommodation for 150 children. The purpose of the Home was to feed, clothe and generally care for the orphans of men, who at the time of their death were in the employ of the LSWR or later the SR, irrespective of grade and irrespective of whether they were subscribers to the Orphanage.

Inside the Home there were dormitories, a spacious dining hall, studies, recreation rooms and a gymnasium, not to mention a modern hospital and large playing field contained in the grounds. The Orphanage was a home for children. There is nothing institutional about it — many of the children have done well in life and it is a place which every former inhabitant can regard as a real home.

Today the Home is being prepared to meet the 1990s; with fewer children in need of help, the

Below:
**The first Home at Jephreys Road, Clapham, was founded by the Canon Allen Edwards in 1885.**

emphasis is being turned to the needs of elderly retired railway workers. To raise funds for better and more modern facilities, the little-used playing field was sold for redevelopment in 1986. Soon the main building will be demolished and one half of the site will be sold, again for more redevelopment, whilst on the other half, more compact accommodation to meet the changing needs of the new Woking Homes will be built.

Left:
**The foundation stone of the new Home, laid in 1907 by the Duchess of Albany.**

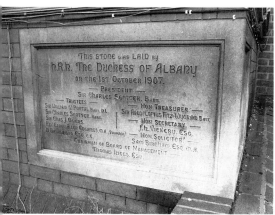

Above:
**A 'new Home in the country', built alongside the main line at Woking. The inscription above the windows reads 'LONDON AND SOUTH WESTERN RAILWAY SERVANTS ORPHANAGE SUPPORTED ENTIRELY BY VOLUNTARY CONTRIBUTIONS'.**
LPC/Ian Allan Library (15876)

Right:
**The decorative mosaic of the entrance hall floor, incorporating the Home's initials 'L&SWR SO'. These initials were also carried on the main entrance gates.**

Left:
**To celebrate 50 years of service to children, a new Thomas Orme Memorial wing was opened on 20 July 1935, with accommodation for a further 100 beds.**

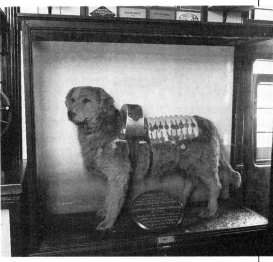

Above left:
**Adjacent to the main building is Grace Groom House, the hospital wing. Above the windows are the dates 1885 and 1925, with the crests of the respective railway companies.**

Above:
**Railway collecting dogs were once a familiar sight on the Southern Railway. Now preserved on the Bluebell Line, London Jack still collects money for the Woking Homes. A medal was awarded to a dog for each £100 collected, Jack also wears three gold medals presented to him for collecting £4,000 before his death in 1931.** A. Ginno

Left:
**To celebrate the centenary of the Homes, a Class 73 electro-diesel No 73134 was named *Woking Homes* during a ceremony at Waterloo station on 19 October 1985.** H. C. Casserley

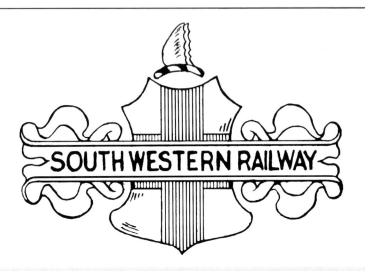

**The Victory Arch at Waterloo; when opened in 1922 it was the 'Gateway to the LSWR'. With the completion of the Channel Tunnel in the mid-1990s it will be the 'Gateway to Europe' — a position held by Victoria station for the past century.**